Former British Judo champion **Owen Lowery** suffered a spinal
competing and is now a tetraplegic. He holds Master's degree
Studies and in Creative Writing, and is currently completing a PhD at
Bolton University on the poetry of Keith Douglas. Owen's poetry has
appeared in *Stand*, *PN Review*, *The Independent*, and *The Guardian*. His first
collection, *Otherwise Unchanged*, was published in 2012 by Carcanet. Poetry
aside, Owen's interests include history, art, theatre, folk, blues and jazz
music, and Liverpool Football Club, all of which are subjects that have been
reflected in his previous work. Owen is currently moving into his wife's house
near Manchester so they can begin a life there together. It is an exciting new
chapter for them both.

Paula Rego, born in Portugal, studied painting at the Slade School of Fine
Art in London from 1952 till 1956. In 1990, she was the first National
Gallery Associate Artist. She was commissioned by the Royal Mail to
produce a set of Jane Eyre stamps in 2005. Casa das Histórias Paula Rego,
a museum devoted to her great passion, storytelling, was opened in Cascais,
Portugal in 2009. She was created a Dame of the British Empire in 2010
and has several honorary degrees, including one from Oxford University.
Paula Rego has had many solo shows of her paintings and prints (lithographs
and etchings) in London and Lisbon and around the world, and has
appeared in countless group shows. A major retrospective of her work was
held at the Reina Sofia Museum in Madrid in 2007 and moved to the
National Museum of Women in the Arts in Washington, DC, in 2008.
During the last twenty years Rego has mainly worked in pastel. Her books
include the Folio Society *Nursery Rhymes* and *Peter Pan* and most recently *Stone
Soup*. She lives and works in London, where she is represented by Marlborough Fine Art.

Deryn Rees-Jones' most recent collections of poems are *Burying the Wren*
(Seren, 2012), shortlisted for the T.S. Eliot Prize, and *And You, Helen* (Seren,
2014), a collaboration with the artist Charlotte Hodes. She is currently
writing a book on Paula Rego and is Professor of Poetry at the University
of Liverpool.

Owen Lowery

Rego Retold

Poems in Response to
Works by Paula Rego

CARCANET

First published in Great Britain in 2015 by
Carcanet Press Limited
Alliance House
Cross Street
Manchester M2 7AQ

www.carcanet.co.uk

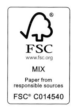

A CIP catalogue record for this book is available from the British Library

ISBN 978 1 78410 003 2

The publisher acknowledges financial assistance from Arts Council England

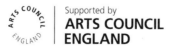

Designed and typeset by XL Publishing Services, Exmouth
Printed and bound in England by SRP Ltd, Exeter

For Jayne

Contents

Foreword

Deryn Rees-Jones

If, as Ernst Gombrich famously proposes, the act of looking at a painting demands a negotiation between medium and expression, ekphrastic poems also demand a negotiation between the image and the telling of the image. W.J.T. Mitchell has thoughtfully described ekphrasis as a tension between the poet's desire for an object, and his or her desire to give that object back to the reader. Presented without the image – which they translate or represent – ekphrastic poems surrender the presence of the visual artefact to language and imagination. They stand alone with the painting as external referent, which can only be recreated, reimagined, or recalled. Presented as they are here, alongside reproductions of Paula Rego's pictures, Owen Lowery's poems – his gifts to the reader as well as to Paula – cannot fail to make us question the relationship between representation and description, the ways in which we look and read.

If, then, Rego's pictures operate within what Maurice Merleau-Ponty has termed the duplicity of perception, they also demand that we read situations that foreground, even flaunt their ambiguities, challenging where we as viewers locate ourselves within a narrative of secrecy, power and desire. A Rego picture will typically dramatise and play with a pause between feeling and action, between knowing and not knowing, between the personal and the political or historical; between what we feel is right or wrong, beautiful or grotesque. Rego's great genius as an artist is the way in which in that pause she allows multitudes of potential meanings to unfold. In her brilliance in playing with the tradition of the male gaze (of the contemporary spectator as well as the gaze of the old masters, of Degas, or Velázquez, say), as she destabilises an authoritative, controlling or even devouring gaze, Rego looks only to make unstable, and to resist acts of looking.

Rego's own use of stories and poems in generating images additionally positions her in a particularly interesting triangulation with the ekphrastic poet. When we read a Lowery poem about a Rego picture which draws its own inspiration from *Jane Eyre*, for example, or when we read Lowery's 'Moth' poem alongside Rego's picture, itself inspired by another poem, Blake Morrison's 'Moth', we are thrown into the deep end of imaginative and gendered engagements with both image and language.

It is precisely because of this that Rego's pictures offer such a fertile place to the writer and the reader, and precisely also because of this that none of Lowery's poetic interpretations is without risk: the risk of reading 'wrongly' by freezing the deep and resonant and multiple significations of the images; the risk of reducing Rego's act of looking to something monolinear; the risk of overwriting transgressive female art with a male voice.

None of Lowery's poems speaks in the first person: the poems throw the self over to the language of third-person narrative that the visual has given us. In doing so the poems speak with a voice of objectivity and authority that is clear and scrupulous but – more importantly – full of integrity. And while these poems are not 'about' Lowery, they are also poems which seek to identify and, carefully and compassionately, to understand; to fill the interpretative spaces that Rego has created. If they do so singularly – and if that allows us also to know the poet – what we find is they know the world tenderly and with a desire to make sense of the pain and powerlessness which in a Rego picture can also erupt into a position of dangerous fury, violence and power. As Rego uses her models – her studio assistant Lila Nunes, her companion Tony Rudolf, as well as friends and family members including her daughter Victoria Willing and her grandchildren – as muses who will stage tableaux as she creates, so Lowery uses Rego's pictures to find a voice to give shape to and make sense of the world, offering poetry as a new form of critical reading. Cross-genre intertextuality need not, of course, be reduced to a simple kind of picture envy or *hommage*. These poems are not intended as a substitute for the pictures, but instead enact a dialogue and set up for the reader what the critic Marjorie Perloff has called (in quite another context) the potential for a kind of 'binocular' vision. Such a vision at its best will always open up the world, and, as with the best criticism, will send us back to the source, the rich pastel colours within the square frames, to our own thoughts and feelings, and perhaps even to our own writing as we read.

Rego Retold

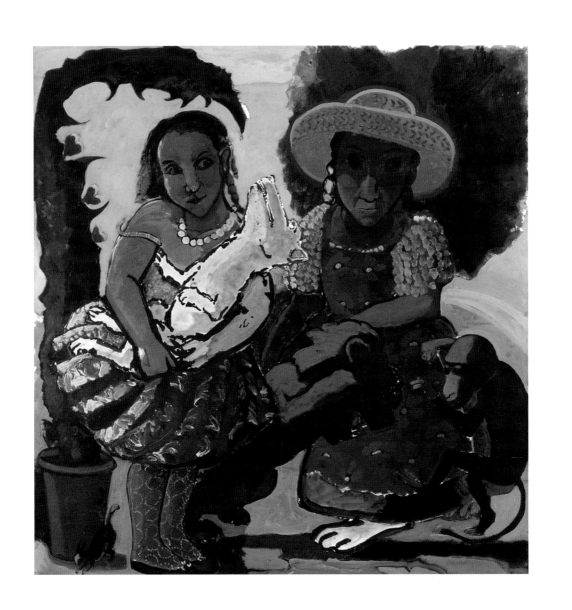

In the Garden

In an afternoon of always summer
the younger woman expects forever
to keep its meaning, to be as stable
as the cradle she makes in her strong arms
for the lolling and chirping dog leaning
into her on its back. For the older

woman forever is only older
than she was in the garden the summer
before. In everything, a leaning
can be felt, including that forever
promised by the remembered grip of arms
around her and the birth-smell the stable

had in the spring in the years the stable
was all hers, and she all his, no older,
either of them, than the now of his arms
and his hands, the first languor of summer
clinging on, the first taste of forever
afterwards on the straw with him leaning

up on his elbow and the sun leaning
in through chinks of afternoon the stable
couldn't ignore. Nor could she forever
as their fumbles started to grow older
by the winter, found their lungs the summer
after filling the void between her arms

with the first year of her daughter. Her arms
grew accustomed to the dead weight leaning
at her chest, felt, for the first time, summer
collapsing, the teetering of stable
concepts of self. With her daughter older
than *she* was when she gave her forever

to scream into, the mother's forever
is as long as the dog her daughter's arms
will not allow to grow any older
than the lank heaviness of its leaning,
its smelling of the straw in the stable
in a longer and a stiller summer

than the garden's. His arms were forever,
and how it felt leaning on straw older
and younger than summer in the stable.

Girl Lifting Up her Skirt to a Dog

He will look, he must. Now she'll make him see
what she's all about, see the woman trapped
in years of greying love, devoted time
she could have had to be the flowers curled

in the shadow beneath her dress. She lifts
the hem, catches the sun on blue and gold
hoops, the backs of her hands and arms. He sits
as an ornament carved to keep him real

once he's gone, the gaze of a child who knows
less than he should. What she desires, she needs,
collides with their yard's afternoon of still
life, courtesies of contemplating growth

as an abstract. Keeping her skirt outstretched,
she kneels and spreads the darkness in her thighs
for him to stare into, to be absorbed
past emerging. His eyes answer the sun

against which her legs become trees. He sits
between the shrills of birds extending claims
and boundaries. A mountain's calm, a cliff's
settles around them. When she moves, the sea

moves. When her thought snaps, it's the brittle crack
of trees when the heat gets beyond them. Birds
scatter at the sound, then return. She feels
the sun beneath her dress, accepts its touch

with her eyes hammering at his. The sun
has the hands of an angel, skin with love
pouring from it. She'll stay like this as long
as it takes to be more than a contrast

where the light hits, make a pool of warmth fill
the hollow in the cotton she can keep
holding out in front of her like a tray
as long as it takes her to make him see.

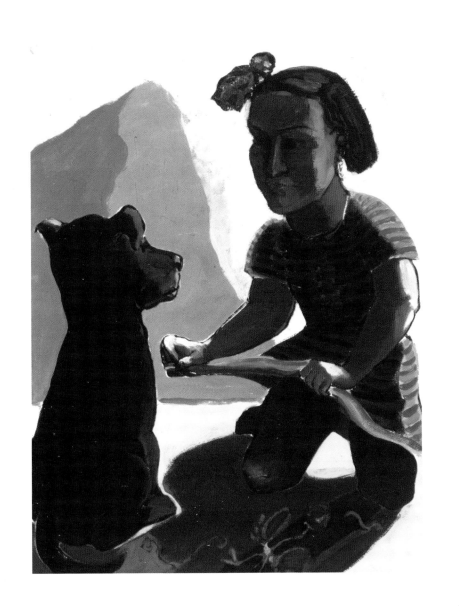

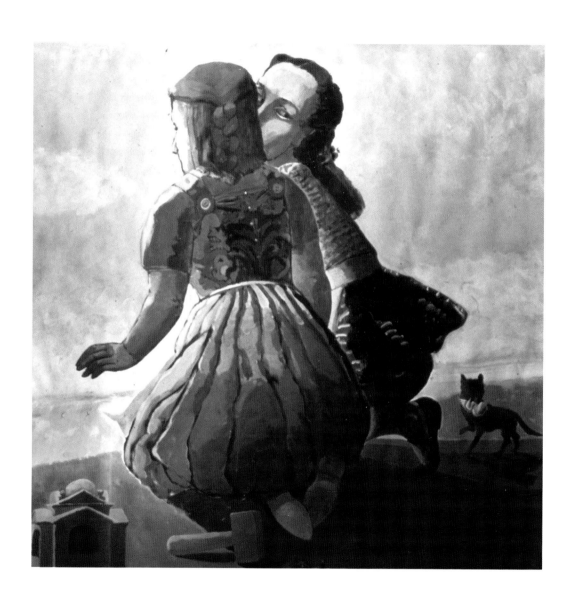

Prey

Their cat copies the angle of the look
back across their shoulders, frozen holding
a dancer's or a hunter's paw at odds
with the floor. One of the sisters' hands floats
with similar deference to an act
withheld as long as anyone's looking
their way. The story's as easy and old
as apples, as the chance a hammer thuds
into certainty before it's dropped, throats
tighten on and swallow. Preserving tact

against discovery, they keep their backs
turned on the world, kneel together, blocking
an evening's light and leaving their shadows
to command the space behind them. Whispers
pass between them, hiding beneath their breath,
feeling the world's stare tickle at the slack
of their dresses. Between them they lock out
conscience and its associated nod
towards any connection more than gasps
at their midnight touches. In the heaven

they've given themselves, anything they do
is theirs alone. Their cat sees, but ignores,
always subject to the latest tremble
in the garden context, the flickering
wing of a lost bird, so readily drawn
from one world to the next. All we can know
here is how completely they fit the laws
from which so much of their sisterhood stems,
how far theirs is an empathy unique
to them. When one of them feels it, it dawns

on her sister too. Looking after him,
they reached the point at which they could both tell
what the other was thinking, when the time
was right. When one of them rinsed her hands white,
her sister's shone as clean. They'll have pressed down
his pillow together, both a simple
matter of effort and weight, and the will
to share it as neatly as kisses chime
across their lifetimes of mornings and lights
puffing out, of dark closing around them.

Looking Back

A conspiracy of glances
protects the common memory
of three for whom truth resembles
uncompromised trust. They'll each dance

tonight as though they danced with him,
in a circle, oldest joining
hands with her youngest sister, coins
jinking in their pockets, shimmered

with the light from his garden's white
moon. The middle sister will serve
as a bridge between age and nerve,
acquired and innate wisdom, bites

on the throat playing at both fear
and love. She, in particular,
arches a good thigh on the stitched
shadow where he lay, somewhere near

how it was with him. Her skirt laughs
all the way up and not quite back
again. Her right hand curls, tracking
him down from touching to the draught

of absent rooms. The youngest hides
an effigy saved just for him
beneath the bed, or else it's him
manifested in china, tied

in a guillotine-red to make
more of his snow and ice. The first
of the three to be all his purrs
across the sheets where he lay flaked

in petals and kisses. Their pause
teeters on the breath suspended
where they'll sleep together blending
half-light into their common cause.

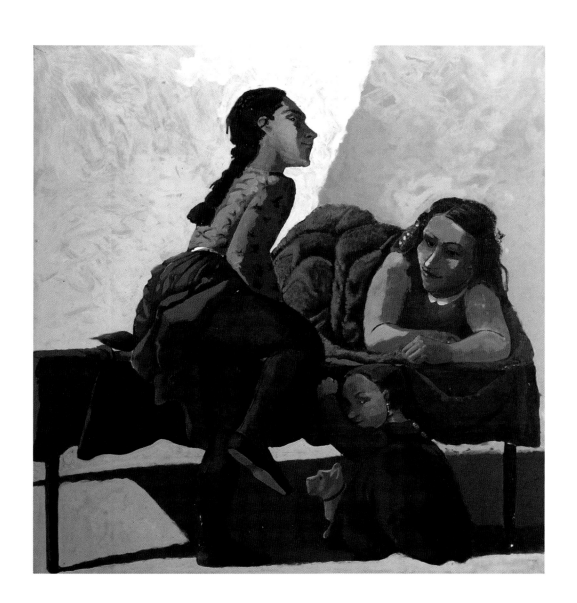

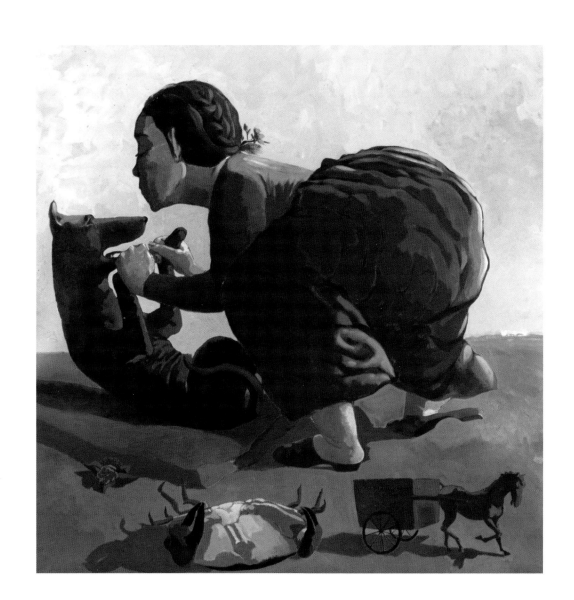

Snare

Her kiss buzzes in front of him
whether he takes it up or not,
an offer at once confronting
what emptiness means, testing what
it might feel like once he's water

and air instead. Closing her eyes
helps magnify the difference
separating how he just lies
beneath her skirt and quivering
breath from the pale tremble of leaves

above their shadows. The dud toys
she's played to death scatter on earth
baked to the colours and noises
of amphorae starting to burst
open. A flower she wore thirsts

like a cut tongue beside them. Heels
slipping from her shoes, she stretches
her pout to his face, appealing
to the chance of her affecting
him, and of his detecting her

as more than a break in the sight
of morning. On his back, his knees
curled, it's so easy to tighten
and release him, to let him tease
out of it, before glass freezes

over his eyes. If she let him
he'd stay like that, a crab with glue
between its shell and the floor, set
like a busy tile. She would too,
in the spirit of the bright new

experiences they can still
share. Her love tires to the wet laugh
the cameras never notice,
too tiny, too close to the draught
between kisses and her father.

Departure

He should be just right
today, ready for the flood
of light, the snapping
and hiss of bulbs attendant
on the chance of nailing him

half-way, gazing back
over his shoulder with one foot
each side of the gap,
the carriage-door hanging there
like a parched flower. Before

his face has time to
react, his default will be
that expression birds
are shot wearing. The photos
can be kept on tenterhooks

a little longer,
enough to have his parting
exactly the way
it was so many more times
than a love counts. His black shoes

must be from his first
interview, his suit the same
as the day she was
an hour late for him, checking
his watch to find it frozen

in its time. Mornings
and evenings ought always
to be this still, this
uncomplicated, as safe
as this for the fishing-boats

to lean across. The stone
of roughed walls and houses hangs
its shadows as still
and dark as waiting to wake
fully knowing there's no need

to now. She makes him
everything she's known him as
in the sun on her
rooftop garden. His eyes close
to anything less alive

than the weight of love
mending him, her finger-tips
saving how he feels
to her, how he'll appear last
thing before his train homes in.

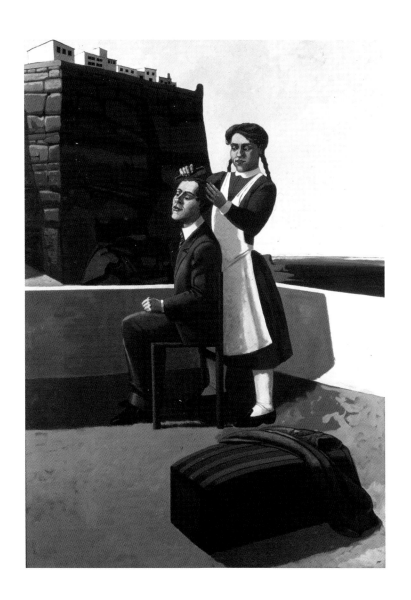

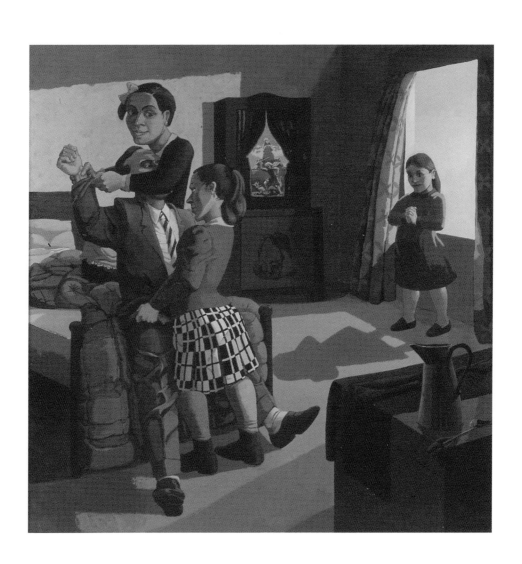

The Family

The stork has a choice when called
upon to pick a bone from the gullet
of the fox. Their picture in shadows
on the wardrobe door adds

form to the dance of an instinct and a need
neither of them fights. Apart, freed
from the circle charred in the grain,
they lope or rise from the pain

of being what they are. Above them
Saints George and Joan in another
play on the same terms
the church gives permanence to

approaching town. The domestic *retablo*
presses the point the lances have stabbed at
as long as the kids have been there
to see their father wearing

away. Longer, in fact, the figures
likely to have been handed down as niggling
reminders of the familiar drama
wrestling with legs and arms

on the bed. The lovers they were look
across the struggle of her fingers hooking
his sleeves up. His answers smother
under her arm as she covers

his mouth and hardly feels it. His best
of course, for their Sunday sharing the rest
of the day after church
and dinner, and also for the lurking

pride of his still caring. The girls
play their part as well, pearling
prayers from the potential the saints
on the wardrobe are tuned to, or straining

to get his trousers straight. Between them
they'll have him right. They'll dress him and clean him
as often as it takes. They'll raise him
as an image in his own place.

Joseph's Dream

If he feels the weight of her watching him
topple further from himself there's no flicker
of acknowledgement, no sense. She could cut him
a double in driftwood or stone, or stitch him

inside his dressing-gown with the same freedom
from interruption. He's seen her this wrapped up
in what she's doing enough to know nothing
stops her once there's a spark caught in the sap

of her eye. Even on the desert road
with the baby in tow she had to stop
for a trick of the light and the parched whisper
in a tree. He's woken to her bolt upright

beside him with only an empty room
to look at and the traffic noise dissolving
outside, had to shake her out of it, slap her
once or twice, before the trauma resolved

and melted clean away. It's a good likeness
she's getting. A mirror or standing water
would be no better and possibly miss
what the page on her easel makes of thought

and any breath he's due to lose. She's hovering
an angel over him, placing a shadow
answer to herself at her most unblemished
and God-filled at a distance from him, adding

the touches that speak instead of remotely
staring back from their surfaces. The floor
around her feet gathers previous flights
and gasps of angels less perfect or fortunate,

and other selves. It's not them pulling down
on his right arm and the shattered step,
the palsy of his lower jaw, but could
as well be. His fingers make an exception

of torpor in the act of reaching out
of sleep towards what Mary's seen already
and captured. Give her an hour and a pencil
and she's all contentment and the same steady

humming through her teeth she always does. Years
only ever change so much of a person,
visions or none. The shapings of his mind
on its private drift offer flashes nursed

from the dark. He watches her fingers graze
across his image, sees what life might do
to them as she draws him sleeping and he,
in whatever form he has in dreams, new

as the morning they've yet to find their sheets
warming to, studies her in turn. The life
will flood back into his hands and his hair
darken and thicken again. Her belief

will return to him and how his hands feel
tracing her, re-understanding the difference
she'll look for and find around his right temple,
the flecks of white his dreaming may have left there.

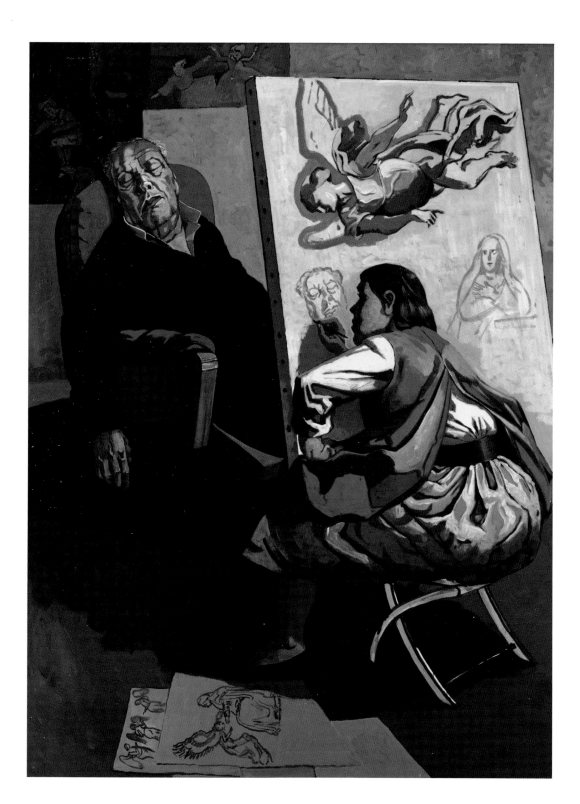

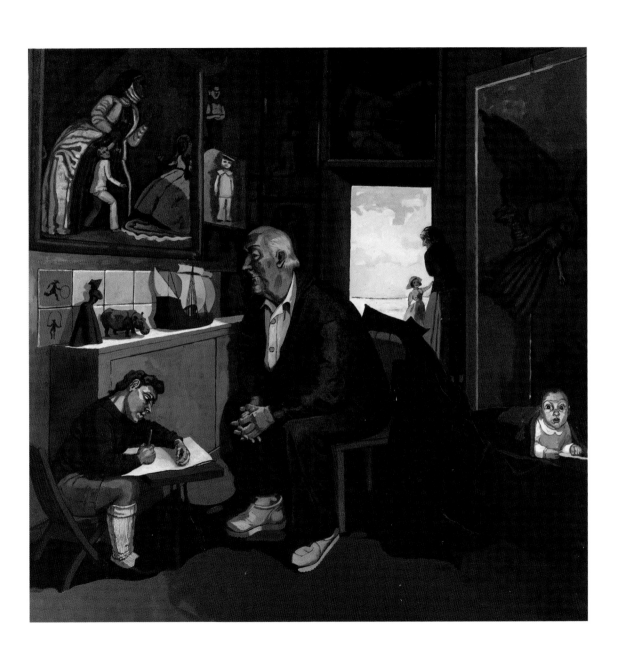

Time – Past and Present

Curling round the world of the page, her left hand
makes a frame to hold and preserve her father
leaning over dovetailing hands. Behind her,
shapes from the shared dream

gowns in blue and white and a head-dress promise
sleep. A nun, a mother, a child-man, tiny
next to her, and led by the mother further
into or out of

space, their tension nailed to the wall above tiles
whipping hoops and skipping. A line of carved toys
make their way from sunrise to sunset, leaning
over the present

where a cupboard serves as a make-do shelf. Time
waits to hold them where they'll disturb reflections
lazing under harbours. The first, a wooden
boat with a stiff sail,

crosses close beside the impassive father
growing more alive by his daughter's rapid
fingers. Second, snouting towards horizon,
rumbles a hippo

wanting out and followed by grace, a woman
decked in navy blue, as allured, as drawn, caught
mirror-eyed and full of the same transforming
light. As the daughter

works, the toys are led through the haze. The room
throbs
in and out of focus. A doorway opens
out to show the girl in another moment
reaching between sky,

shore, and where a skirt and a headscarf threaten
her with disappearing. The far wall shows wings
thick with darkness, hovering, setting night loose
using an angel's

shimmered voice. An infant expects us, judging
by her constant lens. An innate echo
moving in the younger proleptic fingers
makes our intrusion

real enough to stretch to the girl perfecting
concentration, keeping her father's likeness
hers for now, the stare of the moon or starlight
carving a shoreline.

The First Mass in Brazil

To the crushing and listening sea
gathering the fringes of its strength
to let it finish, to the belief
of the forest and the pelted rocks
cranked up a swim from shore, but as much
to themselves as anything, they kneel
on the sand. The cross they've cut and hammered
or brought here with them stands for the moment
against the thickest dark in the leaves
and throws a shadow of its own. *Making*
the most of waits to become another
mantra balanced on divine provision
and expected blessing. For the woman
laid up in her bed with her collection
of effigies and dolls, her hands cupped
around her belly, only the sea
inside her matters now. The wax mouths
of the first flower-heads to be plucked
for vases hold the most recent morning
and the newest rain. Resting her head

on a poncho, she turns from her window
on the shore to face the cool her room
allows and the haven of familiar
streets and villas. Behind her, the forest
edges closer in feathers and weapons
to listen in on the chants and echoes
from the shore. The woman feels them moving
and her fingers make a benediction
out of resting on the bed. The streets
she knew dissolve into the wild hoops
and cackles, the tremors of a raw green
dreamt into life. She could, if she wanted,
heave herself up and waddle to where
the sand gives and burns. Her belly kicks
at her dress. The communion goes on
loving in the sun. The taste of bread
fattens and forgets on her tongue, sweetens
into blood. She lies swelling and turning,
lets the waves gush across her, aware
or not of essential alterations
her eyes sharpen with a darker light.

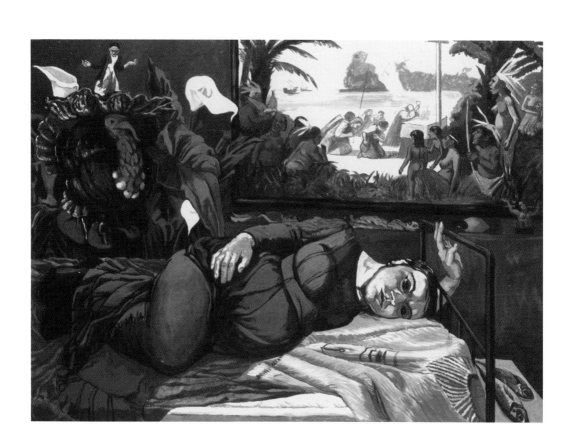

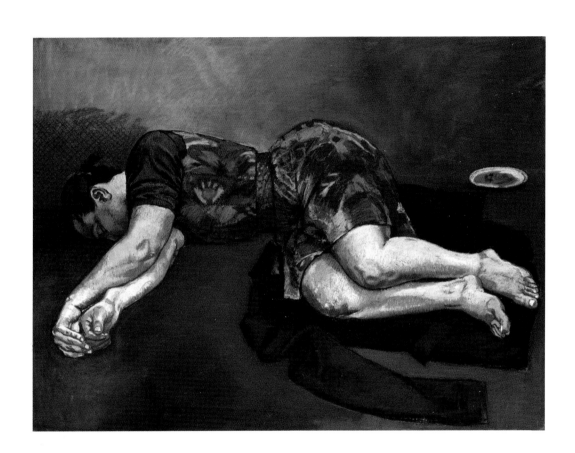

Sleeper

Discovered this way from how long
lying in the space a jacket
holds? Beside her a dish remains
the white of a collar, a lack
of inclination explaining
the food it holds as a hunger

refused. Or as one never felt
growing from what a room becomes
once it's left behind. Sleep expands
in the vacuum, the clumsiness
of arms and legs sinking through sand,
the compromising wealth of pelt

eased apart and not responding
with more than its last warmth. Flowers
grow in the sea of a blue dress
clearing from the semi-gloom hours
have burned to. The calm possessing
her fingers hangs in the fondness

their draping together carves them
into. The touches they received
relinquish from their vague curling
beneath her palms. More like iced leaves
they are, or settlements of pearl
making her nail-beds marvellous

in their working dirt. Her face turns
to its own shadow, possible
thought, or dreaming. No traces, though,
of breath deflecting the glossing
her skin shimmers. Unless it's slowed
to such an extent each one learns

what it means, before the next slips
away. A twitch in the muscle
might kick or snatch at her stillness
on the floor, her lip. And then frost
again. The change, the force her will
falls into, which gnaws at her lip,

catches the scent in the jacket
pressed by her right hip. Images
flicker a shape, a man, the gaps
between him stretching him simpler
than his leaving, her mind snapping
shut on the hope of reaction.

Moth

It had been coming. Hours would pass
without her moving. When she did
rise from the sofa or the grass
her limbs were rusted, like the lids
of old jars. Her food would last her
all day, clotting to the middle
of its china. She'd had to give
up her work to the drift, and live

according to the liquid terms
cooling in her veins. Voices slipped
into the memories of sermons
in an angled light, the dipping
of heads as they succumbed to warm
torpors. The odd word could still rip
through the malaise, sharpen her name
from so much else wearing the same

inflection. But the moments grew
further apart, moons tugging at
the curves of their orbits. She knew
watching cobwebs for the struggles
of flight against the mesh gluing
them in, or down. The mugginess
of summer. And night impending,
dragging itself across an end

from which it would wriggle on red
wings the following day would fill
with blood. She'd not made it to bed
that last time, twisting round the chill
inside her, oceans in her head
slowing to the trudge of hillsides
in floods of ice, her gaze welded
by the ceiling's electric spell.

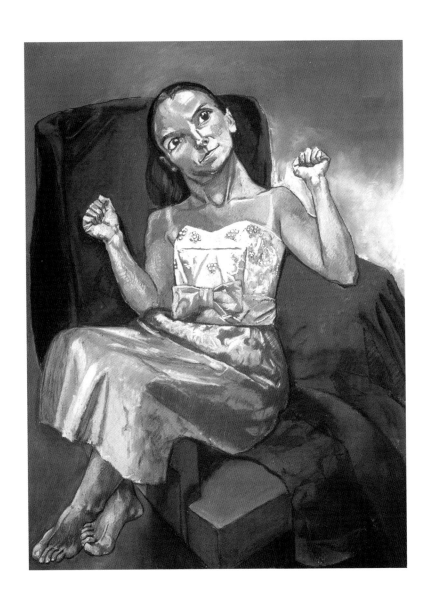

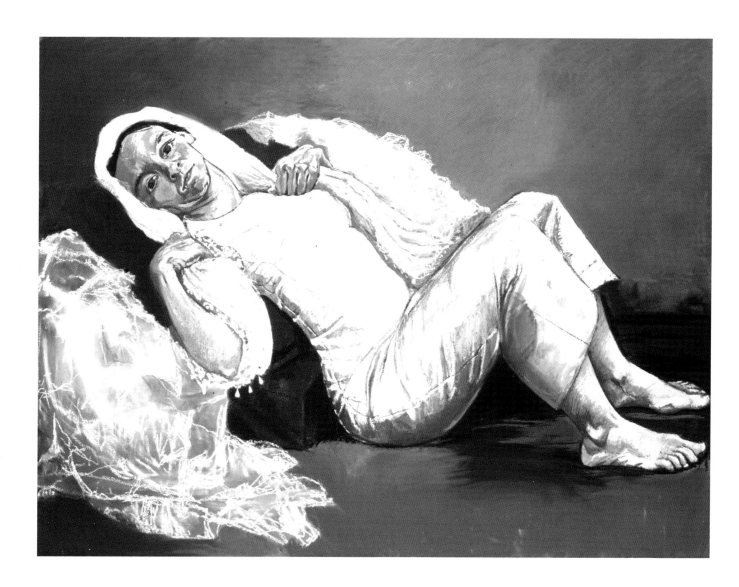

Bride

A morning or evening from emerging
in the shimmering fullness of her colour
by transition, her satin gown sullies
with the touch of light, and all urgency
leached away. Her staring offers nothing
beyond reflection, a mirror's seeing,
or a river's. The soles of her feet warm
to the soil in lulling grass, the sloughing
of momentum to her simply being
aside from the constant beat of forming

and breaking down. There's what hovers before
her eyes and the vacant strength behind her
of a rock, an arching against its blind
resistance. She is shape and withdrawal
towards her core. Her fingers have found her
shoulders and settled there. She lies between
a gauze of wings and the lap of the sun
she'll rise or fall by. Inside is the sound
of shorelines and an infiltrated green
hollowed by a wind-change, late or begun

in the newness of an hour her blood fears
responding to. If the change takes she'll lift
on a leafing breeze, carry on its gift
of breath. She'll drag an afterwards nearer
than the stoop and gather of branch and burst
flower. And if not she'll shrink with the cool
of night and keep her torpor undisturbed
for the following dawn, almost nursing
herself through the compulsion calling her
here, the wing-snap of her first turbulence.

Target

Kneeling stiff and upright with curtains closing
round her, endless deaths and revivals acted
out in drag converge. As an instant opens
seas of adoring

faces, mouths will stop what they're chewing, couples
pry their fingers loose and applaud her falling
almost gently, kissed and then suffocated
under her white sheets

shifting waves of candle-flame. Some might rather
end with moon-eyed Juliet's passion sliding
out of focus, knife in her chest, its memory
pressed in the soft skin

where her palms declare her a lover foremost,
then eternal victim. A cushion mimics
waiting there and spares her the floor's abrasion,
kindness equalling

that of leaving Catherine Howard to practise
leaning down, embracing the wood, the same block
set to catch her splashes. The way she's upright
though, it's the posture

Anne adopted, neck and enchanting shoulders
peeled to show the sword an uncluttered progress
through the bone. The shape of her arms, like
                                        clipped wings
flapping against her,

offers nothing. All she can do from there is
help it, slip the straps of her dress aside, know
what her gesture signifies. Calm, despite death,
wanting to make sure

when she goes to bed with a song of willows
barbed inside her throat, she's got prayers shining
on her lips. With night at the door, she'll manage
somehow to let it

tread its thunder up to the bed, then try words,
try to talk it round. In her stillness, awkward
as it is, her readiness stands the forked heat
better than raging

back against it. Maybe, or else it's difference
found because it's looked for by rows of couples
losing what it was when they fought like hot stags,
lay in their silence.

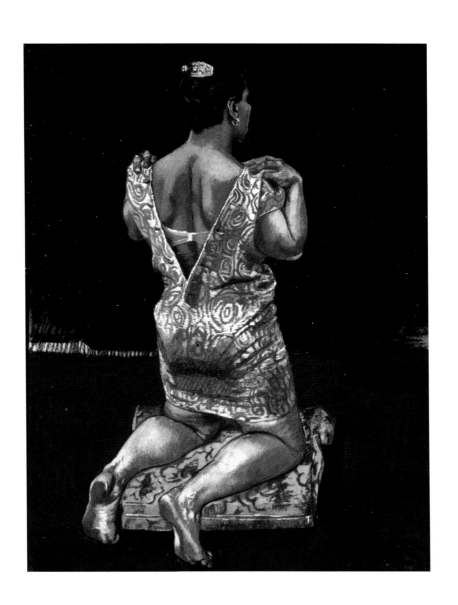

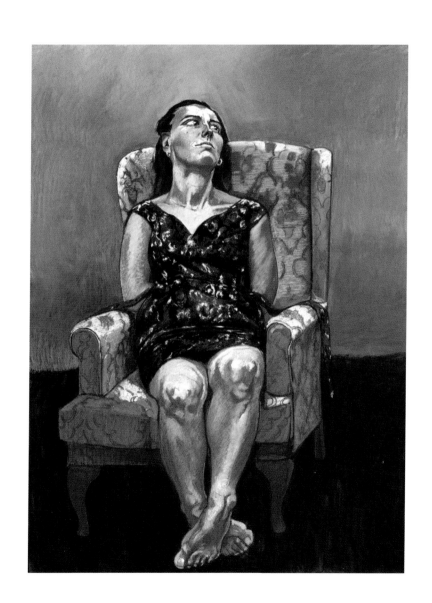

Sit

Her eyes tether to the difference
of his getting up, his heading
this time to the door with the street
beyond. She remains as discreet
as day-lit stars until his tread
crosses from their years of stiffness

into another time. Her chair,
its legs the colour of split thumbs,
holds her to the promise she made
the morning they were paraded
in front of the dead and dumb-struck,
collected in the lithic air

of moths and hymns. Dried coffee stains
mottle the flowers in its arms
for every time her sitting there's
been toppled in her sleep. Wearing
the shape of her hips as farmland,
the chair celebrates a restraint

lifted as soon as the door knows
he's gone for good. Her gaze finds ways
of its own to move, touching books
he'd sit and read, pages he'd look
between, making certain she'd stayed
sitting where she was told, alone.

Snow White with her Stepmother

Everything about the stepmother angles
against both itself and the gentle
touches of pastel she'd happily have strangled

in their pink birth. Upright, or bent
double like some malignant coat-hanger,
she's always looking for the grace that went

sour as soon as it stood with its throat
taut in the glass, gaze fixed
on the polite illusion the mirror floated

out of duty. Love's constriction
leaves only the bones and that elegance
her clothes accomplish in contradiction

to the general theme. And the more telling
detail she's captured in carrying out
to the letter, something they do when they're telling off

a daughter in parts of Portugal, an undoubted
princess in this case, not hers, but made
to feel that way, standing as stout

as any peasant with her knickers displayed
for the Queen's inspection. We shouldn't laugh
at the way it looks, at first, the way

they seem to be the different legs of a giraffe
vying for the same holes. The dance
of stilettos and socks as clumsy as a calf

on its debut takes too many chances
for that. They're only ever a step
from disaster, the clouding over of the glance

looking for love, a self-deception
as gross as any you'd find hoping
against hope in the bathroom, intrepid

in its way, but so ridiculously open
to that counter-thrust in the belly of the maternal
it sleep-walks into an endless scope

for the vicious. Perhaps it's part of their learning
how they fit each other
well enough to be left turning

in their sleep otherwise, the pair of them smothered
by opposite ends of the same need
to acknowledge, or become, an essential truth

they might both, in their different ways, be freed by,
a means of prising apart what's locked
together. The princess, starting to bleed

by now, and the stepmother caught looking
down between Snow White's ankles
for that blush her own cheek's lacking,

both so afraid of an erupting frankness.

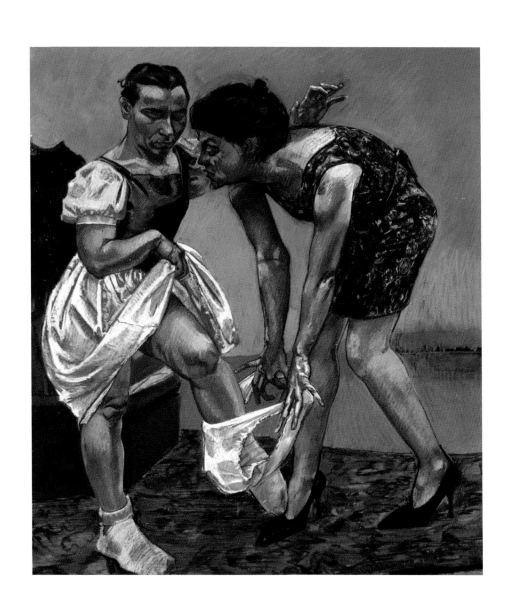

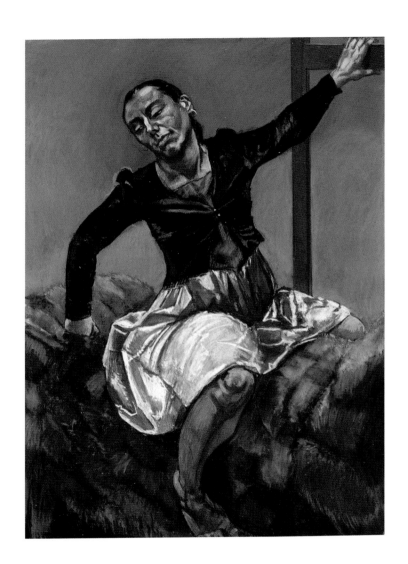

Snow White on the Prince's Horse

Those rider's thighs of hers coax and urge
a dream to move. Creating the life
required of bedding and a day purged
of anything worth being alive for

gets easier with the repetition
tedium breeds. She did see him once,
the prince, as if his entourage wished
into dust, leaving them both the sun

on the rooftops and the street to share
with each other, sporadic attempts
at conversation hardly aware
of their illusion. And then they went

sliding by, floating on the same moment
from its other side. It wasn't him though,
so much as his horse, the muscles coming
true through the sheen. She rocks on her glimpse

of strength between the cascading crowds
with her skirt gathered up, her left hand
asking the wall for support, head bowed
and then leaning back. Thinking abandons

anything that isn't the raw power
lifting her further on to the gallops
outside the grounds. The crack of woods
startles more from her ride and the wall

of flesh and bone her duvet was. Eyes
closed, she pats the damp neck, encouraging
every ounce she can from the rising
and letting her vision explore her.

Two Women Being Stoned

Who they are and what their sins were
matters beneath the dust and blood
of their appointed day, each thud
aimed through the clamour and a din

of birds. Scarlet, the hackle dipped
in war and then paraded calm,
or the moment majesty's arms
drop for the axe knowing the rip

a dress steeped in martyred colour
makes in time, help frame a contrast
with what thousands of years of sun
does to anywhere green. Falling

happens so slowly, like the hacks
by which a tree breaks, or a rock
bakes and splits. A broad hand waits, cocked,
while another touches down, tracks

the laws by which the two are clapped
in the same chains they've worn since red
primed the berries and the first red
apples. The dirt stage spits and flaps

its protests of dust at dulling
blows. The one of the two women
yet to be stooped looks the moment
square in the eye, her hands as full

as the nails she seems to be held
to the sky by, her wrists raised up
until they're cut down. Once grazes
and gashes snap open like shells

and flashes of why, it's a shoot
on a Sunday afternoon. Shapes
are hit and shatter. Dresses scrape
and earrings peck at their neutral

gleam with nicks and smearings. The shade
waits to cradle them and fold them
in its numbing cool. Vultures roll
over them as the stoners fade.

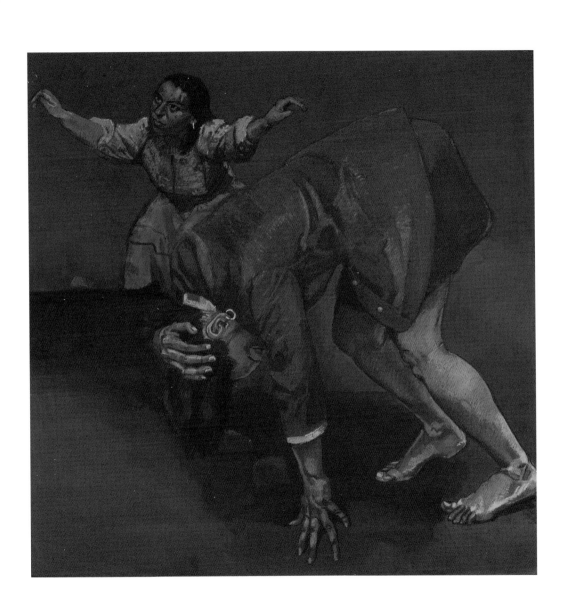

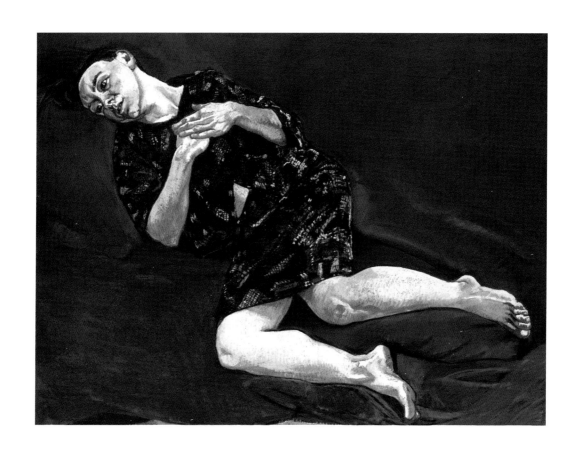

Love

She floats on a scarlet sea of sheet
clamping her hands to the bird she feels
flutter above her sternum. The passing
of days ripples across her and brushes
windows on which she could close the curtains
or leave to watch the show. In the dress
she hasn't changed, a tear and a flash
of skin will have to wait. If her eyes
move, it will be the stutter of flame
on the window-ledge, or the plucked nerve
by which a hen can run in a circle
until its blood runs out. There's a note
around her somewhere scribbled and left
explaining nothing more than she was
and is in love. The light would mistake her
throat and hands for any of the saints
polished as close as prayers and whispers
in the church. Her hips and her strong calves
less so, being more overtly hers
than her maker's. The soft crouch her hips
and knees become is as much unconscious
gesture as the life she's bottled deep
inside her womb. The phone by her bed
is bound to start ringing from its world
apart if it isn't knocked and spilt
across its wire. The sounds from the street
are the bin-men mostly, also wanting
in their way to know why it's a while
since there was sight or sound of the woman
so often up before them. The bird
on her rooftop will watch them a while,
arch its wings, and then tremble away.

Love II, The Dybbuk

Even half a season early
would she sense the weight of a bird
settled like a leaf on her stick roof?

Would anyone until a corner of the bedroom
swells inside its nil colour?

A black umbrella shifts in its wings.
A second look turns its shoulder
out of flight. A dead picture-frame

falls and cracks her lover's face
into a glass kiss. And this is her

instantly filled with the bone taste
of a maribou's bill, its skeleton foot
cupping the roll of her right hip

from the thought of her actually wanting it there
inside. Emptied out that long

when instinct remembers what it was
it speeds the blood. It reaches in
right to the splinter, the hint of white

unfixing from the fleshed end. It fetches
its hunger up to gorge again

on something slipped from the eyes and mouths
of perpetual rows of last photographs.
Wedded to the voiceless world it comes

winging and stiff-suited, pinned
in its ultimate best, boned to the surrendered

breath. It stretches its paper hands,
gapes her name underwater,
shakes in the drowning wings her fingers

dig at. Holding to, pushing
against, the hollow frame, squeezing,

and being squeezed. If they could pull
apart, would the two halves
dive back into the same hold,

neither betraying the sculpted gaze,
all the will of a jug of milk?

But if we could imagine it over, would she
even feel, dare we call it
a dove? ascending from the stick roof?

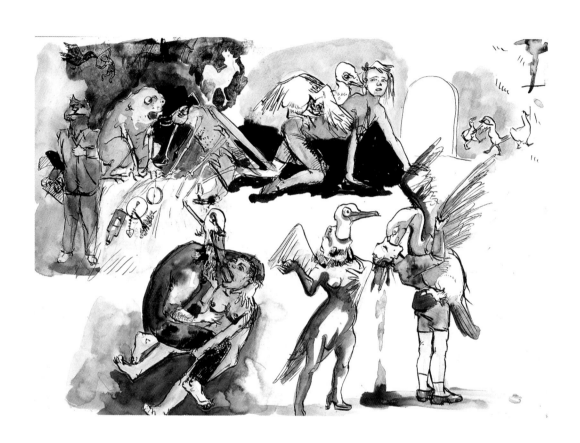

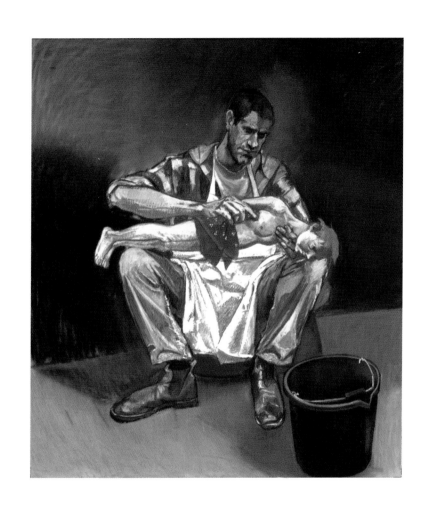

Geppetto Washing Pinocchio

Where his fingertips work the wood a lustre
love alone is entirely able both to
understand and become, the days devoted
to the labour at hand are left with bleeding
palms between their unhurried movements, polish
rags with similar stains. His concentration
grows the closer he gets, aware that pressing
over-hard could destroy the ribs. As tender
as the delicate grain he felt the flinch of
when he held it, without intending to pinch,

by the throat. It's an art, his gentle contact,
every bit as integral, as essential,
as discovering the grove where cherry-wood grows
undisturbed in perfect light and shade, nurtured
by the winds from the south, the water streaming
freshly off the Italian mountains. Nowhere
else it's quite got the same intense profusion;
even when he's been at it days the polish
never gleams with the warmth it conjures up here
under evening- and candle-light. A sap tear

rolls a path from the beads of glass he favoured
for the eyes. It defines a path across cheek,
chin, the moisture around the lips, their gentle
dew and glimmer, as varnish covers each groove
knocked and gouged in. A lover's bruises come true
to themselves in a pulse of purple wing-tips
curling out of the knotted cherry. Fragrance
now of more than the forest. Smells of real life
coming from its internal coma, hurting
with the light in a room of tools, inertia

piled as branches and logs he'll use for firewood
later. When he's exhausted, sweat- and work-stained,
slumped against the acceptance of his best chair,
sounds will merge in his mind with trees in strong winds,
sails and beams, their disturbing. Hooves will stutter
over floors as they try to learn their power,
fingers too, an arthritic dance, as surface
grows from sheen into hard and soft. He'll dream hands
reaching up and exploring his. A hurried
breath will gradually steady to a hoarse word.

The Company of Women

Everything of that swaddled world returns
in his gazing us all the way through
to the glancing water-light of a sickness
murmured soft on the mothering knee,
tracing out the shape of her pendant. As free
as that to find in these others the need
gently leaving him to go feeding
on itself. A reality the dream sticks to
lays him longer on the bed than the room
takes changing to one he's learned

like his first prayer. Resting his stubble
on the lilac of a maid's sewing, a could-be
dress, he hugs that basic shape
his world echoes. He leaves the looseness
of his fingers to the river the skirt bends
against his calf. The hem binds him
in. His feet hang their rudeness
on a nail. Only as a girl can escaping
turn his cassock from war with the solid
weight of obligation, the holy rubbing

of infested hair. These women of his,
they lounge, they tread the safety of the plaid
they've draped and fussed him in. A tease of thigh
burns the roses on the so-not-caring
of a nightie. He finds a place beneath
the incense in their whisper, the secret's belief
in the zest of its sharing, and the way they wear it
buttered on their hot tongues. Sly,
his looking us over from this place where they stay
and betray themselves. Any resistance

he might've had disentangles
an indulgence consistent with the lizard child
curled inside the man. He chooses
now to fold the wound in his side
in the weeping linen of his blouse. How to
hold them so their skin never drowses
from their bones, how to live undenied
among the grazing maids with wombs
the dirt never closes. His smile
flickers an instant at a passionate angle.

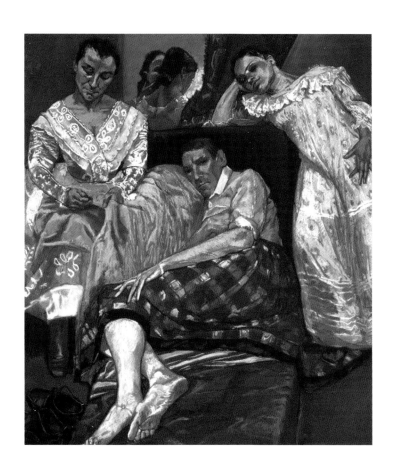

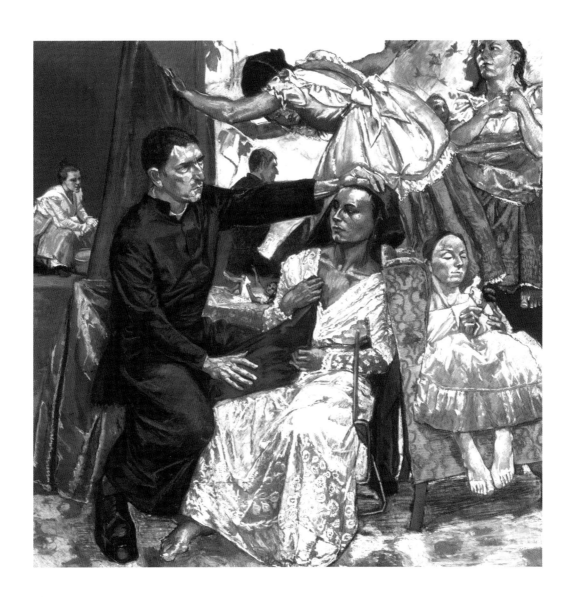

The Ambassador of Jesus

Returning to the scene of those shell-fish days
under the wings of so many women
laced to the sighs. In the black of his business
this time, that attitude he's had to hone
in the bedroom mirror to show him at his serious
best. So much hinges on him here
and the word he's spent so long growing,
that white circle where his throat sits
above the back-cloth. His reflection shimmers
the man who comes from his dreamt haze,

the man with the *perfect* firmly in his eyes,
and in the way his hand falls on an idle
moment further down. That other
she comes to the surface of their faces
now, dresses the prettiest he finds
in the coral blue of the veil, in the blindness
of stone where the skin of an arm unlaces
and he hears the womb-murmur of motherhood
and its liquid world. Not to be denied
his hand on her thigh begins to rise

above itself. The girl, for her part, responds,
pulling away and allowing, giving
the priest her blessing. They could well be alone
in a world of curtains and dolls, of invalid
gurgles. His hand on her forehead, though,
what does the weight of that bestow
as the heat of it presses like a great bell
that won't stop calling? She's shown
so much with the two touches he's delivered
with equal conviction. The girl she was once

before, the dream of her, lurches in his gown
with his whispers and his never laughing as much
as a young man should. Holding the blue
against her skin, browner than the carved
silence his candles so often burn
towards, he'll find a way to turn
her indifference. She'll shine the marble the curve
of a miracle tear, smile the bloom
of maternal grace. She'll be both touchable
and distant, beneath him, and smiling down.

Looking Out

Sunlight, it must be, from the yellow square
her gaze finds a way to reach beyond,
closing the distance with a sentry's capacity
for half watching. Or one of the men
given back by the sea with their eyes
full of a weak and waterish mist
of blue, one of the old fishermen bending
over their lifetimes in the harbour. A massive
universe for her to grow remotely fond of
seeing through, opens the bareness

of a bedroom, any room at all
in which we could find her, and the way he smelt
one of the times it must've been
with the world busy licking at his wafer
and his wine, tarting itself up
for his holy scrutiny. By now her hips
are just starting their meadowing spread, chafing
at her aproned limits. She stands between
brimming over and the first yelp,
the world-splitting animal call

of a shivered sky. Peasant feet
and calves, the taste, surely, of how the colour
bursts from the baked land, of wild
herbs. It's always possible, of course,
she could turn round and, cutting us raw
with her dark fire, slam the door,
all that gentleness gone, all that vague exploring
flinching back into its shell, her child
bucking in her belly like a rubber ball,
the view smashed to pieces. But her completeness

lasts, longer than us, at least,
long enough for the days to redden
by degrees, for her sweetness to lean and absorb,
to be cooled again. Her foot rocks
the seat of her cane chair, finding
a fragment of the tune she's been humming blindly
all the while, the rhythm of her smock
as it trembles. Each tiny disturbance
registers in her elbows at the window's edge,
the knot inside, the vast release.

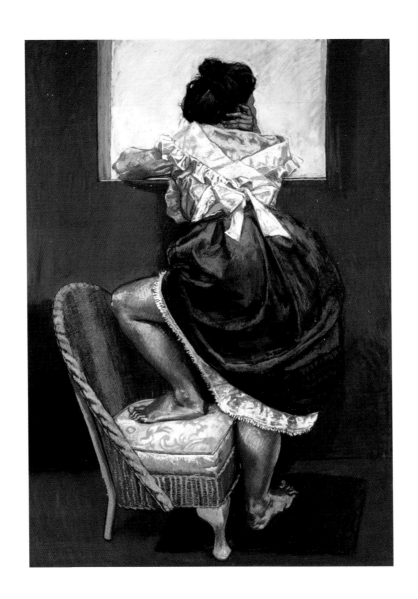

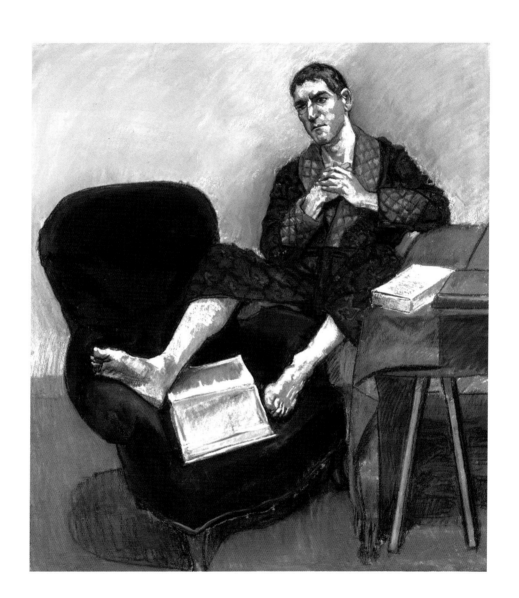

Perch

The composure of hands holding a prayer
to the flicker of its word also resonates
in a face, the picture of a face, from which
we'd never know more than the reflection of the same
thought. Come this morning, or this evening,
his robes are hanging in their joys and their griefs
somewhere safely out of sight, their game
finished for the day, and the hopes stitched
in the black fabric, the town's investment
in their new man, their fresh Amaro,

their latest answer. In a dressing gown
we might expect of the modestly undressed
belief of the self-possessed, if a little
on the fancy side, having found
himself what should be the perfect lesson
for anyone's next time, he rests
his Bible and his feet on his chair. The pounding
in his temples of his own blood admits
her, her breath in the stone, the blessings
rolling from her gaze, turning down

advances, or just impervious, more
ignorance than anything personal. But poised
against the certain, there's the bright *unless,*
the wince in the apple aware of those differences
that might apply to the truly devoted,
as opposed to one of the vintners with their throats
like wet clay, or clod-hops her gifts
would be wasted on anyway, the unobsessed
outside what their ordinary worship enjoys
appealing for. Suspended on these reassurances,

a chink in the curtain has him sitting on a perch
between his table and his chair, as steady
as her, or about to hit the floor
so hard the carpet pebbledashes
bits of prayer, the finger-bright edges
of concentration. Until then, her tragic
glory ought to last, the nebulous
love some sculptor's adoring must've poured
into his best stone, the way that head
of hers never engages with his searching.

The Coop

Past the point at which looking out
alleviates some of their great aching
on haunches the size of houses they left
having to cope and mend and eat
without them. Indeed, past anything
more than letting themselves extend
like apples waiting on their own completion,
wanting one tweak to be cleft
in two. Here purely for the breaking
after the nine months of drought

they tuck in their aprons, they hardly read
between the heat and smell of chickens,
the absent gazing of women, who know
too well, and the drifting further
from the squirming inside in the name of some
lad or other. A farmer comes
sweating for one, followed by a father
for another, with his kiss on her throat slowed,
the strength of his overriding conviction
she might fulfil that soaring need

of his. They'll talk them all to dust, him
included. Made her what? Made her
wrapped in the blue of a shawl. Made her
try on that untouched look
as well, turn her face to holy
stone. Said it was a joining of souls,
he did, dirty sod. Books
are picked up, and as soon laid
aside, the stories already degrading
before they lie on laps brimming

over. Somewhere he ought to be burning,
placing his wafers on the pink tongues
of the bedtime prayers. Judgement rolls
around them. A stretch, a waddle towards
a piss in the corner. So much for listening
to all those urgent words, as if the wrist
wouldn't do them. Like continents explored
past boredom and back, they drift on the wallowing
seas inside them, on the knowledge they belong
nowhere more than where gestation turns.

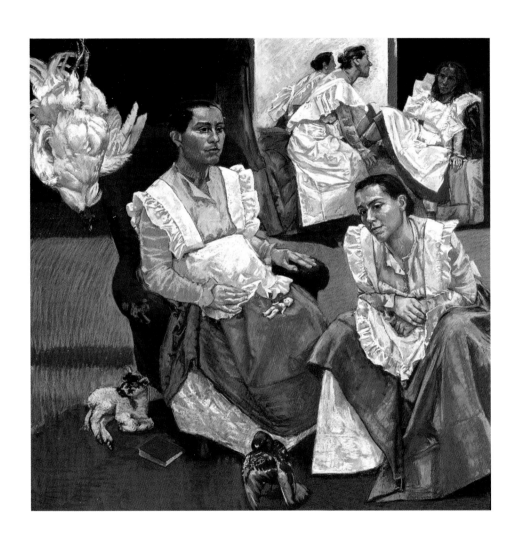

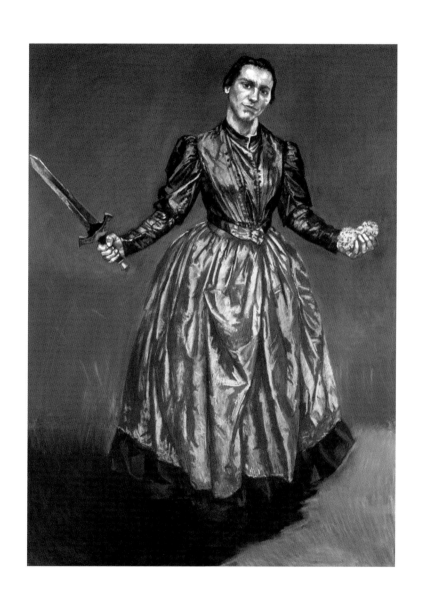

Angel

A face reflecting what it reads in us
prepares to deliver with either hand
the language riding on a sword's tongue,
or the curious blend of wine and gall
drooling from a squeeze of testicular sponge,
something for the hollowing shout, the hunger
in a lover, a mind instantly enthralled
by a promise sweeter than it was long
enough to taste. A shadow stands
to make Her the solid bone and muscle

of sexual choice. Assuming She speaks
it's likely She'll opt for the broken voice
spawned in the thick of the other's coming
into spasms of life, and death, and seeing
how the difference runs from Her like a rose
drowning in its own sap. If She goes
as far as remembering, if Her mind seizes on
glimpses of a timeless past, She'll summon
a less grubby birth, the poisoned
joy of knowing the nature of that unequalled

sacrifice on which She'll bring her sword
shining and slicing down. In a moodless
clinic life will be tearing at the purple
of a cord, the formative hints of a body,
and the gum will be wiped from a forehead, a woman
frozen with sweat. Unless She's automaton
right through to the stare modelled
on ours and the consciousness only of disturbing
a brevity that matters like burning wood
to its black shell. If She's heard

what they say about places like this
being where they make little angels
She keeps it locked behind the glass
gaze. One, or all, of those
lying inside out on their skeleton
beds awake enough to tell
might be touched with the impression of a rose
lit internally, and of their own passing
almost as a sort of distant arrangement,
a disentangling of their human mystery.

After 'Marriage à la Mode' by Hogarth

Part I: The Betrothal

This looking of his with his hands tracing lines
less simple than they were, it comes heavy
with so much of the father's privilege,

the gardener's, stroking the first shiver
he's grown himself with the sex of a finger
purring on its side. She knows he's breathing

that bit thicker by the rings
of dew on the constant mirror. Hung
over his little girl he sings

in her ear that song of theirs she's clung to
drinking sleep from his finger. She no longer
pretends she doesn't know hunger

rests a hand precisely where the fondness
fills his thigh. She knits him in her own
more cloying hands growing strong

with the snap of apples. They're creatures now
contracted by a cord. One moves
the other. His hand on the down-slope

of his thigh could spend a lifetime hovering
there. She teases a foot through the fur
of her dog, sees how much he loves her

just for the thought of it, always sure
it's a touch that can only ever be theirs
outside discussions more undeserving

of the same purity. In the centre there's the sharing
of a pair of mothers, graveside polite
in their heels and furs. *And he shall be hers*

rests on an eyeless boy in his silence
on his mother's arm. *And he shall be hers*
without a thought for the father frightened

back inside the mirror. A nerve
tightens a flinch of breath between them
tied to their deliberate glance, the curving

in the fur of her peeled foot. The queens
might talk their wealth for hours
quietly turning a little greener

based on the reach of their respective powers
to make it a more certain world. The nights
shall be her father's though, and his dreams of flowers

breaking the soil-skin with their tiny bites.

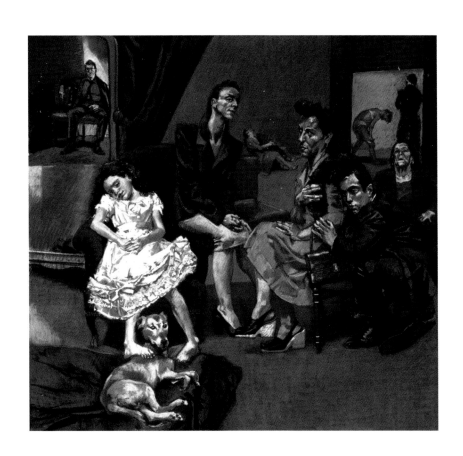

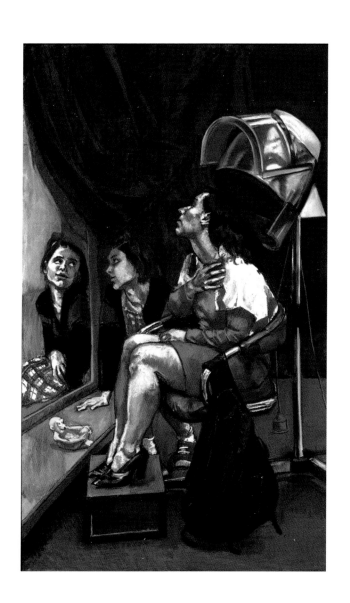

After 'Marriage à la Mode' by Hogarth

Part II: Lessons

Again, they never escape the mirror
gluing their images inside the glass
shrine to their first desires. A year

or more since the marriage, and he's the past
already, unknown to the pane holding
what he's left so hard. The girl's gone pasty

without her answer from the mirror. But we're told
her mother-in-law knows her enough
by now to grant her some of the golden

rules. How to wear her hair, the stuff
she'll want to know if she wants to keep him
nearly happy, if she wants him after

he's found Brazil. It's what people
tend to learn. It's what makes them
who they are. The messages keep on

washing up and all in bottles more vacant
than the last. She watches how they catch
the light, how well they break

apart. Or is it a ghost she's watching
cross the glass sniffing at the flowers
in his green-house, loving their stretch

and their baby's glow? The mother-in-law
adores her hair-dryer and how the warmth
uncoils her there. She pushes her pout

to an echo self and whatever comfort
she's lost besides. The hand on her heart
could be anyone's who never comes

from the glassy stare, never startles
through the door. With the girl it's a different stare
bored away at by the pieces of her father

who never comes there any more
either, except in those sharp flashes
of a sometimes look. They sit on the shore

of their shoreless room, they sit where the ashes
settle their remaining odds. That boy
of theirs, he'll return or not. The lashes

should be painted to curl their buoyancy
against themselves. It's best to seem
compliant. It's what the world enjoys

in a woman, what they're all dreaming for.

After 'Marriage à la Mode' by Hogarth

Part III: The Shipwreck

His depletion lies in the arms of love
divided by the cost. He's the look of a Christ
de-crucified, exactly that lethargy

leaning back on her knees between the blisters
of his cases and his trunks. It's salt we get
coming through on his skin, the gist

of years of seas he's been tasted and rejected by
washing up as a lank white
loosely established in a wax setting

she feels the cool of. All the brightness
their room had paints a way
to an iceberg world drifted out of sight

of this perpetuating ache of metal, its wasted
grey. She holds him as a tree might hold
the frost. And he, in his turn, plays

the part of the returning ghost folding
in on its sense of loss. His arms
in particular have got this emptiness moulded

to a T. Blankets swaddle him from the harm
he's already swallowed by, to the point
it's drooling down his chin in worms

of dead cold, the drips anointing
where they kiss her hands and the softer skin
of her wrists. Is it there the disappointment

can still re-become the simple-
as-summers girl with dreams as full
as her father's were of her? Glimpses

bequeath her a parakeet where the drawers loll
across their tongues. The future's in the now
squatted on the floor as a negro doll,

or in books and a journal the words have drowned,
or been blown from to the groans of their hollowed
vowels. A ladder leads them down

to their frozen selves. Wooden, dull,
always the same sense of falling
under the motion of a passing hull

tumbled and churned inside its walls
to beams and a dance of tangles. From here
it's pointless the petrels stopping to mewl

as they plough the distance between their eras.

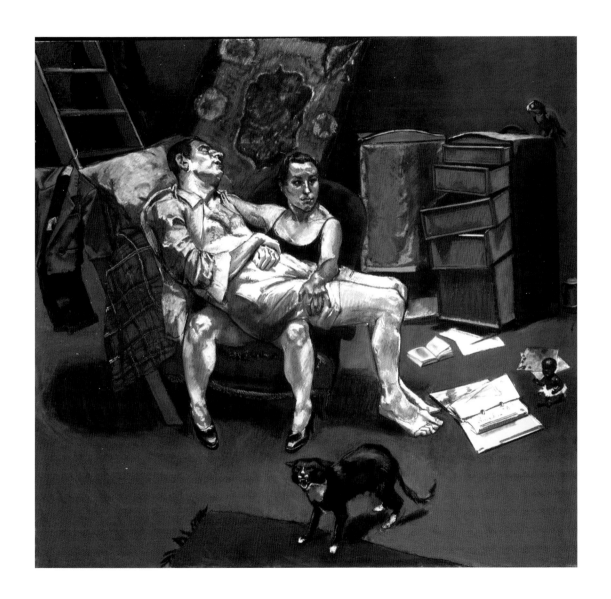

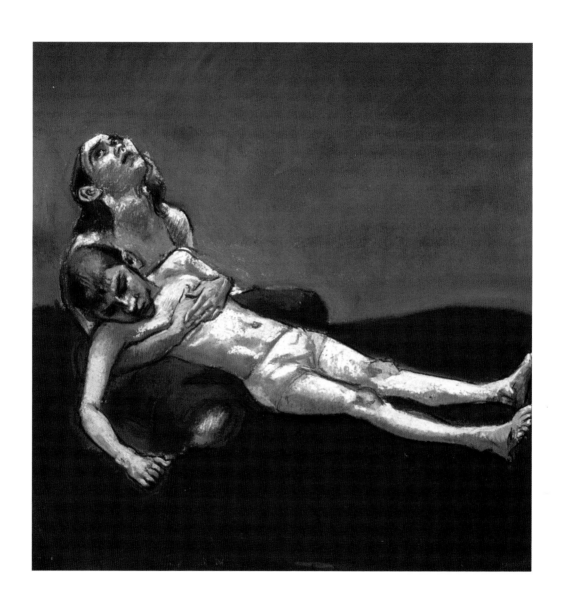

Pietà

She might've known. From the tearing
last night in her dreams, she might well,
but with so much else to deal with
and the knife in her womb to bear,

sometimes the obvious misses
its point. No mistaking now though
the weight of her boy-man and how
cool a body goes as it's kissed

to stone and before there's daylight
to warm it through. No warmth tonight
though, for all the sky's road-kill light
matching her drenched skirt. She'll stay here

with her cracked Pinocchio clamped
between her thighs, her gaze burning
the sky a new hole. When she turns
him over to the others, lamps

will fill the hillside with the reek
of hot oil. But they'll have to drag
her off before she can stagger
down to where they'll end up seeking

him in three suns' time. Her nail-marks
will keep holding him, even hours
after he's been wrapped in flowers
and spices and his tomb's been walled

shut. Nothing, hardly a murmur
between her fingers as they wrap
themselves round him and as they trap
as much of him as they can. Terms

are made and accepted, offered
and lost. Clouds clatter into light
as their faces are carved, bitten
to the landscaping bone. His cough

before the ghost left him, her scream
once she knew, flicker on their lips
and skin. Anything less ripples
into nothing and the torn seams

of her curtains and her bedding
when she's taken home, when her eyes
are too full of the way the skies
just hung there as she cradled him.

Assumption

As enthused as trees when a bolt disturbs them
from monumental dispassion, sets
their remoteness burning towards the transits
of birds and butterflies, Mary arches
and trembles. Here's as alert as anywhere,
given hills are already closer
to that original spark than bedrooms
and towns. The girl in her eyes could stay
with the sky exploring away forever
and grass behind her to sweeten lying
and gazing out of her mind. Returning,
she'd glow, her face like she'd run the miles
from the mountains. Had to be love, the faces
at home or working the market reckoned
the times they saw her with eyes as full
and as wired as waves in the sun. The voice
in her head was sharper and clearer then
than the days she'd bury herself in work.

An impression brought on by having relative
silence roaring the slopes to sea-shells.
She knew that, but an illusion worth her
indulgence, just to be touched and feel
as alive as now. Or as when she melted
inside and knew it was real enough
to be swelling months on, to wipe her blood from
and taste her birth-pains on. Drumming wings
in the thundered grass, like the shores she walks
when the crowds are gone. And the cry His lungs
had been torn by shaking with life as soon
as she held Him closer. His musicality
ringing still as innate and true
as it was the first of their mornings. Lifting
her head she hears and accepts the patterns
evolving round her. Her body thrills
at the presence sitting beside the vertical
tug imploring the sky towards her.

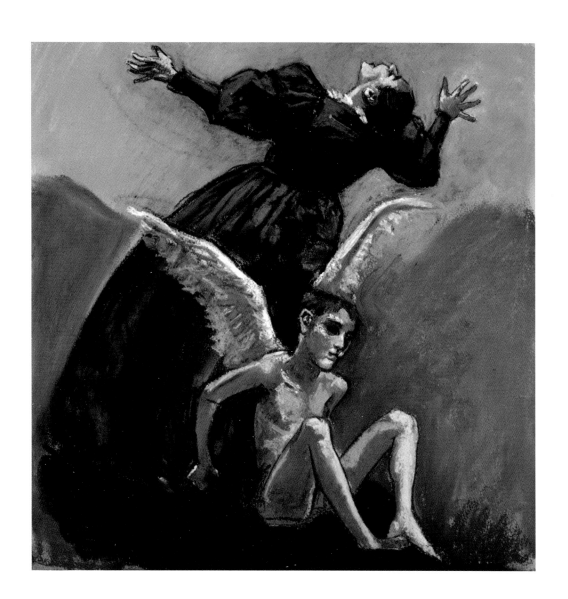

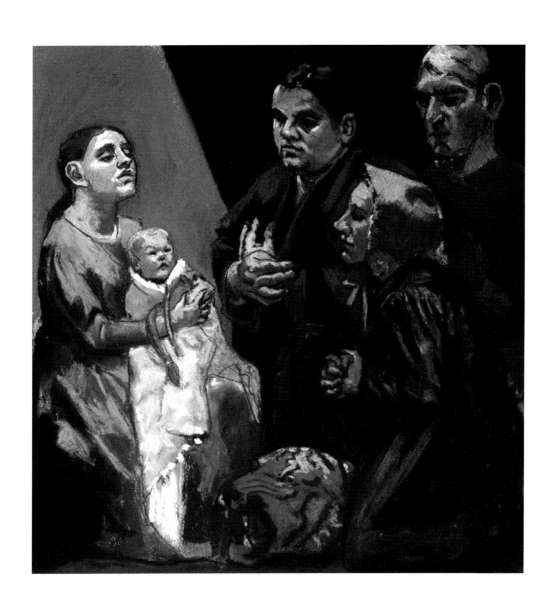

Adoration

Their faces bathed in the warm transmission
obvious miles and days from the drowsing
curve of the mother and child, they stand
or kneel. The first's a woman who crossed
herself and the threshold in one. Branded
with travel and working for the basic ambition

of her fields, she folds her fingers in front of her
chest and partly closes her eyes
against the light. It's that or it's tiredness
makes her. The second's a man who cries
more than her, who's been so wired
to the vision he woke with and wanted to hunt

down, she had to force him to stop
and sleep. Even then he lay
with his gaze as open as the smears of stars
seeing nothing apart from the day
he knew or heard was coming, like bars
of sun the clouds can only cope with

so long before they trickle
out. His hands express the tremor
of a dove catching its breath in the space
beneath his heart. Both shimmering
between their joy and remorse, faced
with that absolute their waking dreams expected

their words gum in their mouths. The stinks
and murmurings of the room, the movements of silks
and furs, rise above their normal
calm. The mother has her blue and her milk
white, the look of a recent trauma
the cattle outside are still shrinking from

in their pens. The third who waits and knows
as much and as little as the rest has work
about him too, the greater reticence
of a man accustomed to the backdrop and the darker
corners. His hands at his sides, he waits
his turn for the boy for whom the seasons slow.

Lamentation

Vacant skies return to the dark of metal
where the women wait on the hill. The people
there to gawp have melted away, the hammered
heat of the daylight

rippled out to traders with stalls to strip down
after hours of profit, the decent takings
days like these can bank on. The cross is colder
leaning against it

now the body's peeled from its lording over
miles of dust. The matted and billowed powder
swept across the pavements and rocks has given
up on its warmth too,

ashen now, the stuff of the mountain caverns
dotted all the way from the desert's one road
up or down. Sensation adjusts to losing
contact with sources

barely understood as distinct from mornings
broken off from love, or from staying too long
close beside a river. The two who loved him
most have his absence

burning under every kiss. They share him
as he was the first and the final moments
either saw him moving between the shadows,
pausing to shed words

over winos stretching their blankets. Lasered
through to who she was in her heart, the younger
mourner remembers how he moved inside her
after her punters

left them talking hours to their echoes. Loving's
cost the elder too. In the mirror only
embers last of what was a beauty famous
miles from her village

in its time. The skies are the mauve of knowing
sunsets flicker out in the end. They'll get up
helping one another when only leaving
matters beyond love.

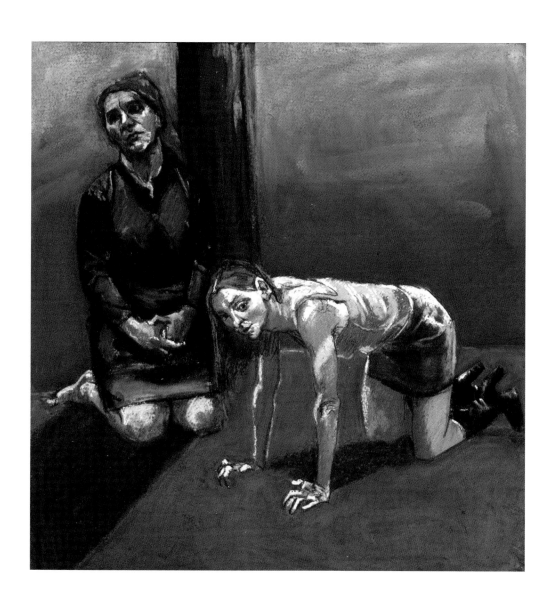

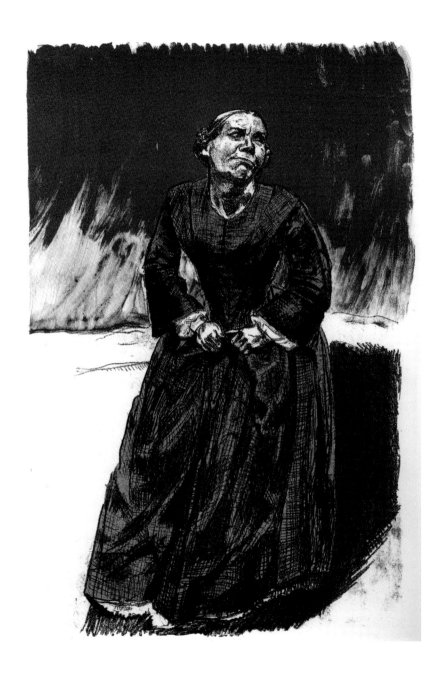

Come to Me

Knowing as much as Jane does
of life before inferno
cleansed it from inside its lust

has to be part of the turn
she makes and yet doesn't make
freely. Staircase whispers, burnt

in the chance mistaking them
for more than they seemed, the pull
under that unshakeable

calm by which she's been moulded
since her school, carry further
than their keyless room. The hold

still of His wedding unearths
the jasmine smells of moonlight
on bedsheets and the split surf

wriggled in the sand of tuned
bodies. There's always something
of a love survives its noon

of bells and flowers. Summers
pass into wanting summers
more. The nail-marks of coming

come to intoxicate, come
again to a pulse of red
from dirt thought to be humbled

by winter. If the treading
up and down on the stairs was
from the fever He wedded

and left to fossilise? Loss
escaping from the tower
with eyes kept impossibly

live might catch its power
by reflection. Why not leave
Him there wound up in His hour

of silk and palms? But belief
could play some part in the clench
she makes of the unrelieved

dark of her old gown, its stench
of the puritan martyr
demanding re-invention

so much it tears itself. Heart
calling across time and space
to another heart, starting

the second one like a chase
of birds. That's how it's written
and how it looks unlacing

her religious reticence
far enough from Thornfield Hall
to lose the last bitterness

of the bonfire. The re-born
penitent calls with a voice
He knows breaks like a morning

on Jane as she makes her choice
on the moors. Jane can find him
in a walled dark which enjoys

how tasting her reminds Him.

Mr Rochester

A forthcoming, from its pool of shadows up
by angles of covered bone, to her knowing
it would happen on a day like this, the supple

terror of a horse's eye holding her. She slows
to the scream of being locked in the Red Room
with its reek of dying flowers, throwing

herself at the door with horror assuming
form behind her. Or not her recent uncle
at all, but the girl from school she warmed the tomb

for in the morning, she lay beside for as long
as it took for her to fade. The dark mass
of a horse balances and shies, hung

both with reins and their froth, sees her dazzled
to a stand-off. It's the gloom's rider who'll crack
the silence first with his anger's elastic

submission. To which she'll fling a coolness back
at least as soft and hard as his, then hear him
sliding towards the relative distraction

of another scenario they'll have shared
by the time they reach their destination, paths
leading to Thornfield Hall. It's easy once the gears

click them more alive than standing for the halves
of the same mountain. He, in particular,
fixed to his finding her an evening after

she dreamt him there, looking down from the flicker
of a blasted tree, from his top-hat's coal-seam
and answer in his boots, his whip-hand's friction.

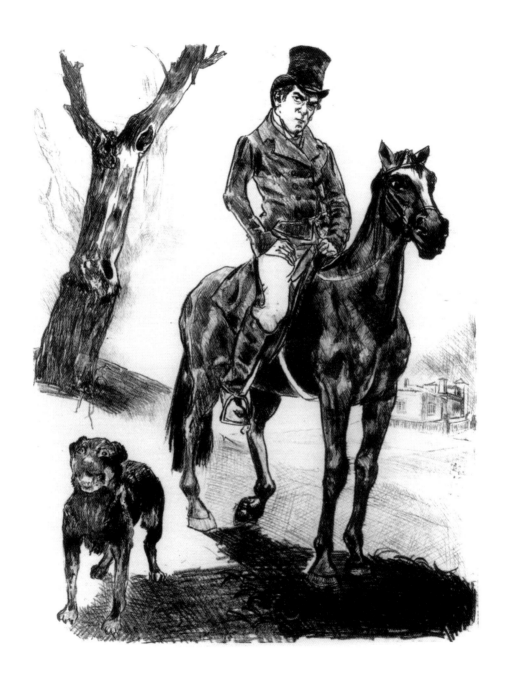

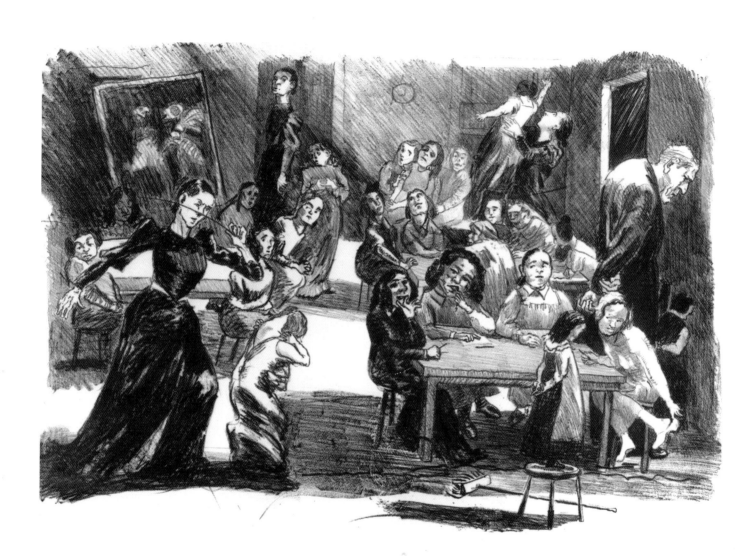

Schoolroom

In a shambles dusting the chalk of lessons
interred as much as acquired, the swish
of a birch's flailing at skin and bone,
at a neck displayed for it. Counting up
to a dozen, sheathing her eyes from contact,
or else compelled to the watching brief
of a wood surrounding a battlefield,
we've the girl it could be. Her sewing slithers
between her fingers, as witness grows
to an anger hanging on childish truth,
an innate response to the gold and red
of a gull-beak, drawing us in. A sharing
of sight, possession as much as anything,
making dark in her eyes reflect
in our own. On squinting, the dark's a dress
with a greed for light, with its polar opposite
finding life in an arm begrudging it,
as the switch-tip above the neck
of a passive schoolgirl expects the next

and the next on gentler and softer white,
a more human white. And a second darkness
with shoulders crowed, and a crag's intensity,
turns its face to the wall, as inward
as graves. We see in the terms the witness
allows, with privilege mapping pain,
a demand as well, a conscription grown
from a whisper medulla-deep. Reflecting
the burn of landed assaults with weals
of her own to match what appears and glows
on her schoolmate's neck. As a twin in need
of a fulcrum, Jane is that definition
a tree-top sways to, but fixed to principles,
knowns unable to stop themselves,
an impression wanting to happen. Out-reaching
too, transmitting across the waste
of a heath and catching her girlish voice
as a lover's question reverberating us.

La Ligue des Rats

Precociousness swells the girl
like flags curling open, words
gestured into more than sounds,
an expounding which she stirs

from nothing. Her poem takes
her up, making more of her
than the collection of nerves
and bright surfaces so raw

so much of the time. Posture
adds its gloss, affectation
learned, she says, from her mother
in that other life she graced

only just long enough to pass
it on. Mastered, it gives her
an instant maturity
reaching forward out of life

and jarring as it does, ice
in her voice, possessing her
at a genetic level,
with its severing caress

already starting to test
its edge. Dressed in puritan
observance and practical
shadows, lagging and withdrawn,

Jane attends as governess
and discovery, that of
what getting herself this far
costs. Her scars tickle the black

robe of her stoicism with
thoughts of knowing a man's throat
arching up over a shirt
hoarse with thirsting. Then floating

from her again as the words
she's heard growing resonate
every mimicked syllable
through her zealous confession.

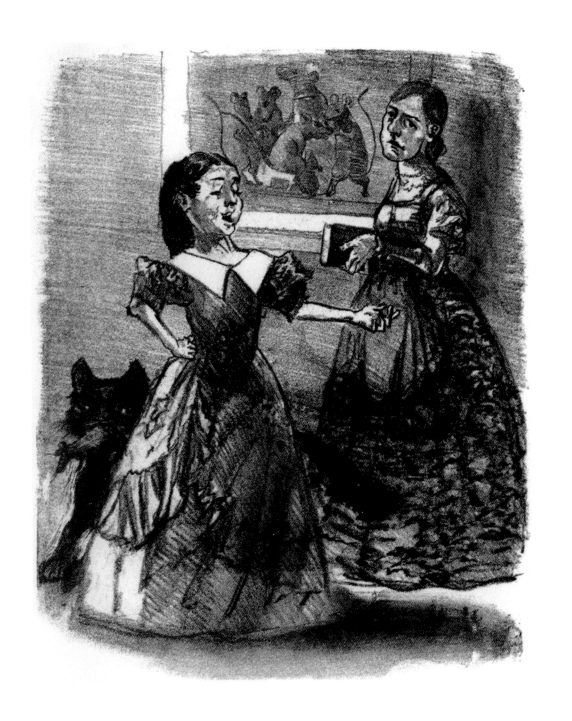

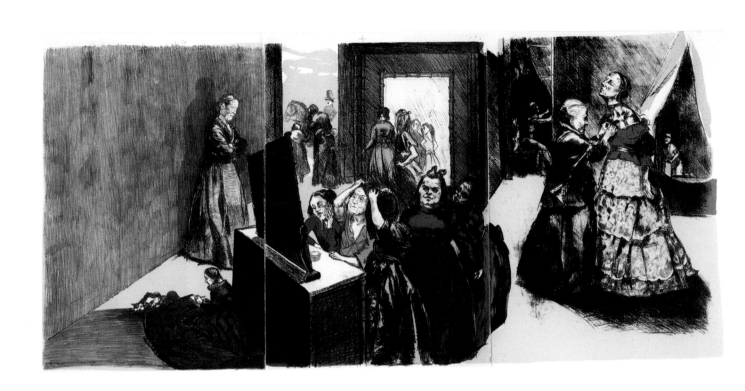

Getting Ready for the Ball

Daylight slices the weight of walls and polish
brooding over its years of wood. A top-hat
arches backwards, prepares to dismount, catching
light when chinks are permitted by the weather,

boots as quick to be touched alive. A stinging
lash of sweat has the hall's embalming posies
running. Roses and honeysuckles, jasmine
winding down from the stairs, its own impending

shadow, feel its intrusion. One who could be
Edward flickers a second still, until silk
starts its rushing again. The ladies worry
mirrors down in the changing-rooms, their gooning

like enamel from water's dark, their gazes
mauve and hollowing. Corners catch their preening
unaware of its being watched. The fringes
peel from curtains on maids with beaks for fingers

pinning ribbons and frills to order. Voices
also, shrieking like nesting-grounds, the same need
deep inside for attention, fascinates more
seen for what, in its rawest state, it is. Cliffs

know, and shores, when it's over, waves will still hurl,
smash, implore, and the pebbles hiss like bacon
fat, the way they'd have hissed before. The fragments
after shells will be clawed away. The cackles

empty out of the doors as sharply as that
too, the difference beads of mottled resin
show to eyes. From imago through to adult
takes the space of a night, and gone, transforming

only what they've alighted on, and only,
even there, for as long as they were noticed.
Autumn suddenly warms on boots and horse-pelts
cooling off in the next conflicting breeze. Dreams

lose their legacies, watching shades and corners
notwithstanding, that is. More native colours
take a day to revive. The shuffles glide back
upstairs, dragging their shrouds of distant flowers.

Biting

Through the layers of coat and shirt,
in a second she finds herself
a vein to draw on. Eyelids hold
her pleasure tight inside their lines,

drinking it in. The weighted life
of distant flowers gushes through
the feral scent of man. The haul
of waves, their pause, their stretched elapse

waits to crash down. The fingers cupped
against her breast become the dead
glow of moon and extinguished stars
fucked and fucked to their final burst

over sand, over silk. They'll close
the door on her room, on her world,
rush bandages and padding on,
watch them colouring up. They'll close

her down again and make her dark
as her Sargasso's sudden plunge
out of daylight. And when the crowds
have filed back to similitudes

in their different rooms, the stairs
will betray where a brother's step
becomes a lover's hand attuned
to the nerve locked behind her door.

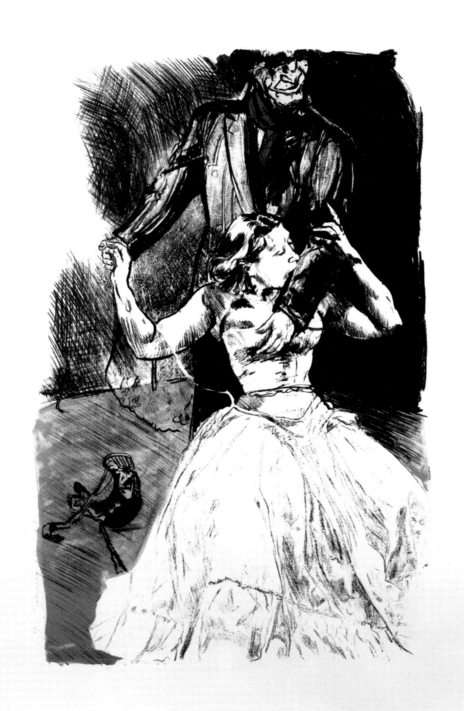

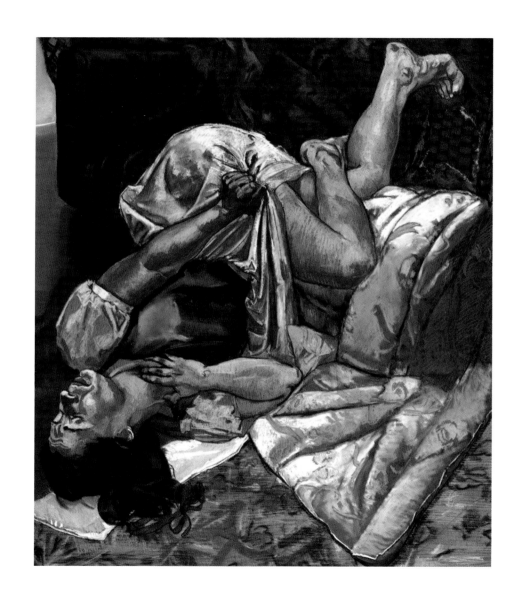

Snow White Swallows the Poisoned Apple

The right hand resting on her throat
affects the nervous habit of a speaker
for whom the words required are suddenly remote,

for all the prepping she did with the speech
and the mirror the night before. It's placed
as softly as the thought it seems to be reaching

for inside her, regaining a grace
she lost as she went, warts and all,
to the floor. What it hides and displays

at the same time is that sense of falling
over a taste with a thorn buried
in its skin, an illumination enthralling

what it alters with a touching awareness
as her other hand tries to mend
her skirt, that thing she's so scared

the world might call her, her self-defence
once the arm and the fingers seize
in their throes. You'd need to make them extend

by force now, gradually teasing
them open a joint at a time, and even
then there's the problem of the legs freezing

in the same way, the body heaving
itself off the floor in parts
where the struggle's clinging to that grim belief

in her youth. She'll be cooling now, her heart
clenching like a stone. There'll be a smile
that simply can't help it starting

to wake to an altered world, a while
before she's found, and they can close the book
on a life they want to be seen filing

past, pausing, but only looking
as long as it takes to see it's true
what they say about her keeping that look of

never quite knowing what to do
with so much beauty until it was fading
out. Among the mourners who go

through with their private dramas paraded
for the crowd, comes one hardly
able to stop the joy invading

her public grief. She'll stay by the marred
expression a while longer than the rest,
study the mouth in particular for the scar

left by the spiked apple, the best
and the reddest around when she walked the garden
with the thought in mind waiting to be pressed

home, to lie on her lips as they harden.

Olga

Olga makes a ukulele tiny
with her hands. The tune her fingers strangle
is carried on an eastern wind blinding
the memory with smoke. From somewhere hanging

further back than anyone here can tell,
she found them one day, appearing to need
food and work. Her clothes are losing the smell
of travel now, a new form of freedom

to try and explain with her thick tongue caught
on the words. Fond of children, she said. Good
to see and hear them laughing. With a thought
she couldn't quite articulate, wouldn't

perhaps. There behind hunger's ageless face
and eyes, Olga knows better than she did
what makes the children tick. She replaces
what she came from by the day. And the kids

sometimes understand her now. The daughter,
more than the boys, listening that bit harder
when songs emerge, ones she's never been taught
at school, but with tunes that once she's heard them,

stay embedded. Olga's thumb is a fuse,
a cocked hammer, set to fall on the strings
only when the shrill in her head chooses
to let it go. Any moment she'll bring

the weight of it crashing down on the sound
of a garden in the sun, remote waves
raising bird-noise from the lush expounding
of the shore. Her voice will rise as wavering

from the dark. Distances from that black earth
her hands knew will close. When the sun reaches
it will be with winter on it hurting
where it touches, where its white edge bleaches

heat on the tiles' sienna and the red
dirt. Olga's voice will come again as long
and deep as ravines, her throat-bulge unsteady,
like that dress she just doesn't belong to,

the wind that brought her from birch forests.

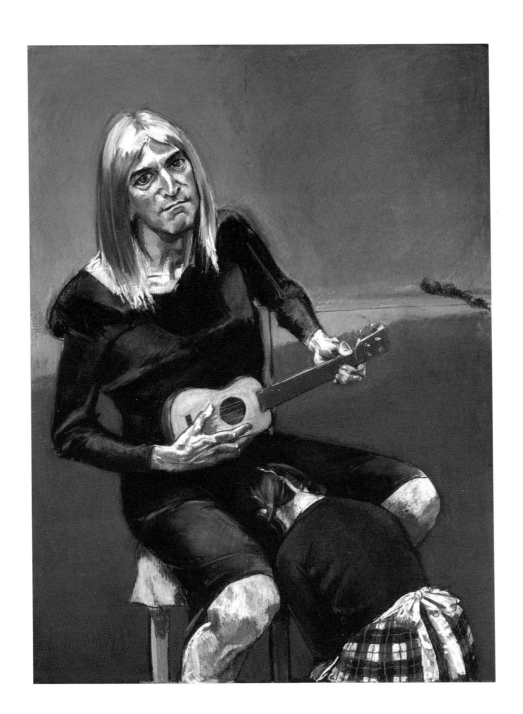

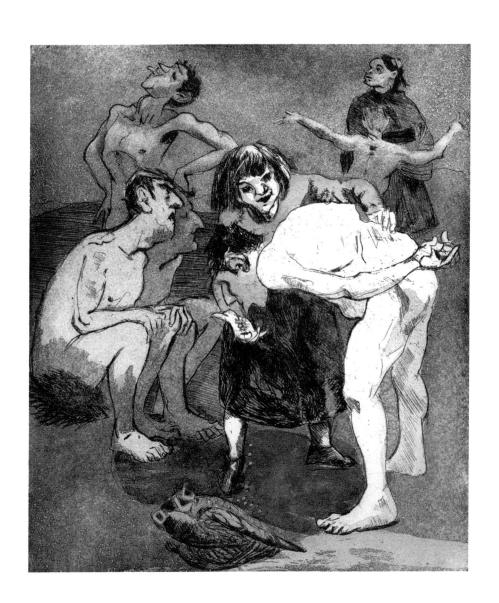

Feeding

Once she's tickled awake by a streak
of sun, she washes in the sink, stretches,
pulls some clothes on, and leaves the stairs creaking
behind her. The buzz she gets expecting
as she approaches the coop and peeks
in on them never wavers, protecting her
from having to face the mirror's latest
inevitabilities. The waiting

between times deals with itself, with more
almost guaranteed every morning
now she's got them trained. If they ignore her
they never last anyway. They're born
for laying or the pot. It's a law
as certain as the light and the path
worn down the garden from the kitchen
and back by generations who've picked

what they can from the clutches, who've fed them
handfuls of grain in their turns. For her,
they produce their best though. Her voice steadies
any nerves they might have, almost purring
to calm the general clatter spreading
from her footfall. She beckons them forward
and holds them one at a time, affording
each the same amount of love. Their words

stumble out from somewhere lost, return
to their knotted tongues. A mumbled thanks
tells her that for a second they've learned
their way back to who they were. Their hankering,
if it is, seldom lasts. The spell burnt
into their bodies and their minds yanks them
up to their roosts again to drop eggs
in the straw between their crooked legs.

Fame

Music apart, the bars and tavernas
are pretty good for the skinny girls
teetering on their heels, flowers burning

behind their ears. Where the dark uncurls
and the beaches become themselves blessed
with space and time, his mornings come early,

like the first winter branches to flesh out
into bargains with the sun. The taste
of the night before, the girl he guessed

a way inside, has already wasted
to the crumpled scent lolling and lapsing
on depleted waves. Tonight's will last

no better either, once he's been grappled
soft again. There'll be the same old rush
reborn, and the subsequent fall, tapping

the same need, with the chances, as crushed
before they start as ever, she was
more than one of his better dreams pushing

through the crowds of those he has and loses
and hardly knows. It's so free and easy
when he's got their favourite songs bruising

his finger-tips, when he can release them
from whatever ghosts they keep between
their thighs with a few more bars of teasing

falsetto. He doesn't even mean
some of the nights he has. But by morning,
if they stay, they're never her. He's seen her

by fractions enough times, caught on thorns
brushing past, leaning for tips at punters'
tables, stood and watched the beach for more,

but always left empty-souled and wanting,
echoing the parades of gulls any
one of which could have her eyes and taunt

as well as her. At the bar again
another salute of glasses tilts him
a vow to be the closest they can

to how her teeth and talon-marks felt
before the space beside him, the light
pouring in through the window's gape, wilting

across her flower-head's broken petals.

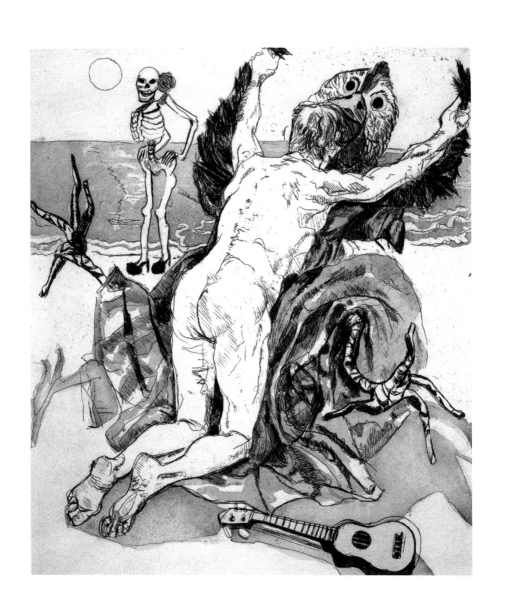

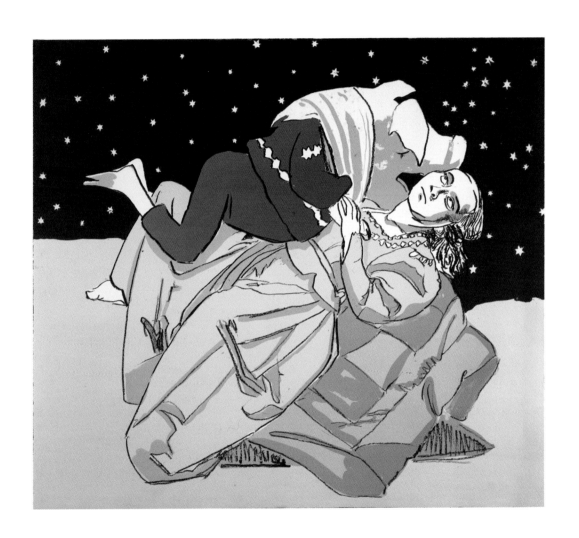

Prince Pig and his First Bride

Carrying the weight of his curse and wearing
his Sunday best, the boy with sandpaper
skin and a farmyard smell follows
the path assigned him. She laughs, then seeing
the wound splitting his fondness and his pride,
takes it back, tells him he's better
than he is, listens, whispers in return
offering love for hurt. Holding him
she can relax a little, lose herself
to the canopy of stars expanding past him
into a dark forever. When she shivers, she's clever
enough to pass her repulsion off
as the chill she always feels outside
of an evening, knowing he'll believe her, and go on
believing with her hairpin lodged in his heart
and his sigh stuck inside him. His sucking
and licking, his thick breath, his heaviness
dissolve in a second. His neck stiffens
and then spasms calm. Once you've walked
a thing like that through in your mind
it's as good as done, the only difference

being the squeal, like a kettle, or cats
fighting in the yard. Hardly married
a month, and at her mother's request, the rest
is just force and time. He fumbles at her and falls
into her, grazes her shins. His face
presses against the prettiest dress
she could find. His tusks grind and muscle
closer, exposed by the ludicrous kiss
his lips can't manage. They'll stay tangled up
until it's over, the stillness hovering
above them, a sullen cool rising
and starting to clot. Uncoupled, certainties
will remain for the morning papers to pick
apart, the pale of her body, her pulse
oozing out of his tusk-marks and tarring
the yellow of her gown. Telling gouge-marks
scurried in the dirt from tracks deeper
in the forest will breed fantastic stories,
along with the obvious legacy he'll have left
for the luckier crows and foxes to dispose of.

The Psychiatrist

The pen assumes control of its own
momentum, only using his fingers
as a prop, allowing and encouraging
letters to form the name of the woman
beside him, connecting her with someone
she lost en route. The loops and curves pour
across their boundaries, forming rings
that come increasingly close to honing

down those extraneous layers built
of all the times she's not herself. Red
in a certain light, ink glistens letters
as opposed to shapes only in moments
of brightness between the mist that comes
sweeping in behind her eyes. She's let him
see where she's seen herself, and he's led her
back to the windowless room they fill

with their time together. Or she's clouded
over for their entire hour, sat tight
with her feet crossed and her toes like ice
against the tiles. This afternoon answers
his opening questions and advances
towards the shadow starting to rise
across the wall behind her. She fights it
as long as she can, tears the black shroud

wrapping her in dreams from which she can't hide,
the ghost of a child who never speaks
more than the single word, *Love*, the mother
figure dried to the scent of her white
hair. As the pen carves across the brightness
of the psychiatrist's page and hovers
over the wound inside, it starts leaking
out through her dress. She feels the heat sliding

from her in waves and the room receding
into the greater softness where years
separate and drift away. The child
watches her with constant eyes and turns
and fades. The mother figure, too, burns
a while and then disappears as mildly
as she came, leaving her echo there
between the swirls of ink and the bleeding.

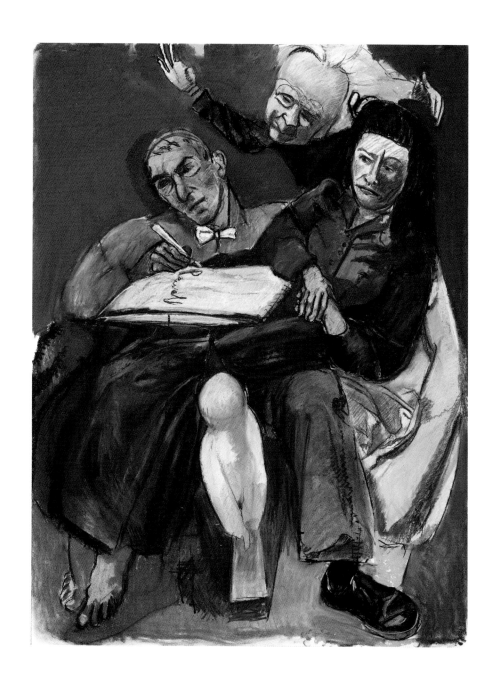

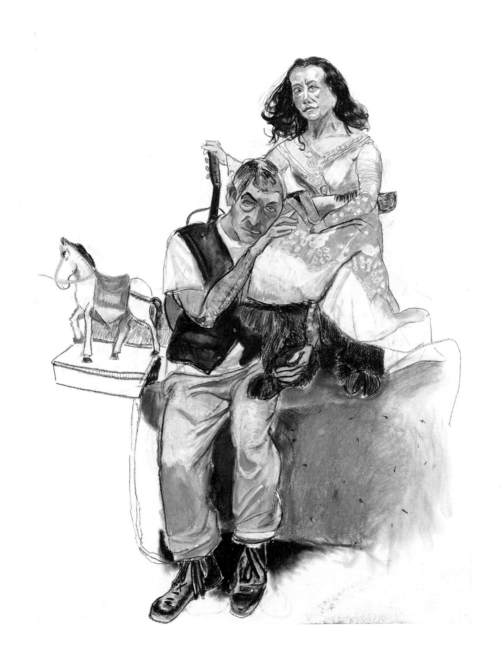

Dame with the Goat's Foot (I)

She'll allow his right hand and his head
against her thigh, his mesmeric stroking
of the heat inside her dress the freedom
it needs to let her know. As a token
of loving him back, she'll murmur needs
of her own down towards him. The broken
parts of him will mend, settle again
to the lulling sea and shifting grain

washing over the remaining glimpses
of who he was. Before will lie sky-watching
in a gentle sun with a flute simpering
out from where the fields and the dunes rise
and fall. His world will be made on simple
and edgeless terms, muscled curves of thigh,
finger-tips, when she feels like, to stir
his hair, keep him lost in their recurring

and revolving dream. On either side
of them as they are the shapes of people
will blend with their shadows, split on tides
spiked with light, the lap and dazzled leap
between flanks of wall or shore. He'll slide
deeper. She'll no longer need to keep
watching his face for signs of resistance
or his eyelids for more than the gestures

he's there at all. There'll be a point soon
she could stand, ease his head and his hand
from her fur, and go. The feral tune
of her body when it moves would tend
and nurse in her absence. If his loneliness
knew or felt the change affect their landscape,
the flicker would soothe back to wild milk
before he knew. But she'll stay with silk

where his face presses the dry hair flat
on her thigh and with his pulse a nail-end
or less away. They'll have the dry crackle
of her pelt between them, his hand trailing
from her knee to the bronze shine and clatter
of her hooves. The daylight will turn pale
around their love and waiting for her
to let him, to make him with one word.

At the Table

Their monolithic silence stands
for loving dry and curling back
to where the loving tasted thick
and strong. The stillness wants to brand

them each as lost as Manet's jades
with eyes for absinthe only shared
with needing cash to keep it theirs
and stay as lost as stars. Displayed

the way they are, there's no attempt
to reach across. His stupid hands
are inches from her knees, but strand
themselves on his instead. Exempt

from their pretending any more,
she's safe to let him wait, to not
expect or hope she'll soften what
the years and fights have settled for

between them. When he shone she burnt
her fingers wanting him. His silks
were nearly new, as fresh as milk
and money, jokes their loving earned

about their being wine and fields
of wheat, the whiff of cedar-gum
and fur. Her voice was clear and hummed
the show-tunes with conviction, wild

to spite the world she fell from, worlds
from his, she loved reminding him,
in case he ever felt he'd climbed
towards her. Neither looks, like pearls

engulfed in fleshy hazes, sweet
explosions dredged from how they were
for real. The wine's its own deserved
remorse as well, but that's as neat

as sousing gets. There's nothing left
to stop him simply drifting off
to mope outside, or ghost the love
of other tables. She could give

herself to anyone she liked
with wine enough to dose them with
and still some shape to boast of. Live
until you can't be arsed to kick

arriving here instead. The nights
they really didn't care, the dark
electric buzz, become the marks
of having seen and loved it, slight

erosions where the water slid
behind the dark. If either speaks
before their time, or either seeks
the other first, the magic splits.

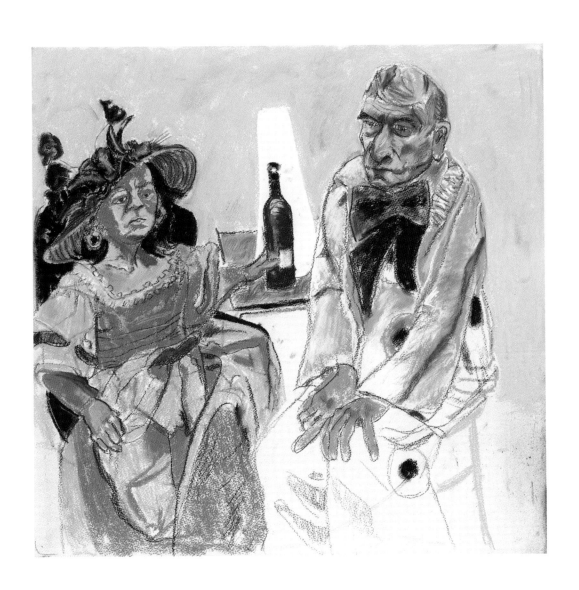

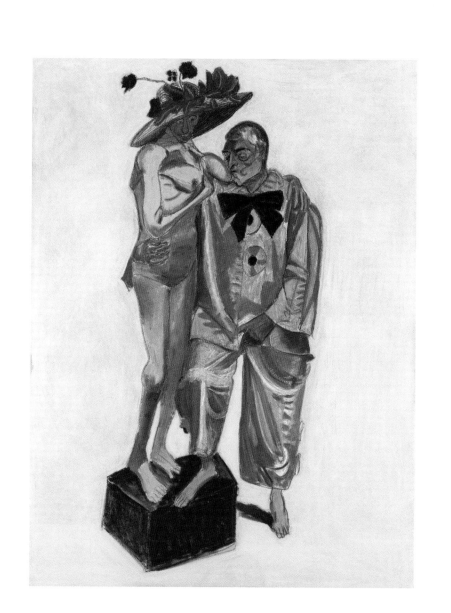

The Last Feed

As tender as the first trickle of colostrum
out of love and duty and the loss
neither of them felt stinging
at the time, her hand brings

his mouth closer. He takes from her
gift with the same lips and mumbled
prayer their earliest nights
heard themselves lighten

into. His hand finds an anchor
on her waist and the way it curves to a flank
of skin on bone. Her flesh
manipulates into place as he presses

forward and rests on the white powder
of her breast. Around them the bedroom flowers
burn beneath their swaddles
of dust. Her fingers mould

his collar-bone strong and young and the satin
of his costume as fresh as the wet tatters
love's tumbled down
for years. She could have drowned him

in love once, looking at his face
stripped of so much erasure
does to anything warm
and real. It's more than comfort

and the hollow need isolation
remembers by photographs and the flickers of places
where they lay in colour
breathing like seas and the lulls

between them. She's his life again
and the moon he searches for when the pain
swells. He'll forget the one
who cut him and feed on the sun

in its last hours. She'll be a Columbine
for him as long as he can taste the summer
on her and his costume keeps
his wound and his silence weeping.

Flayed

When he gets it right a single sheet
pulls away in his hand. Revelation
gets personal with the skill and sweetness
harnessed to the same uncomplicated
movement of his fingers. As he neatens
his operation, she's face down waiting
on a cue to resurrect, the must
of the sofa they've shared for years clustering

like wilted flowers. She felt it coming
seeing him increasingly distracted
again, lost and constantly encumbered
by a vision that left him contracted
inside himself, answering benumbed
when she tried to drag his passion back
from his bootlaces and those horizons
he watched in the walls. Between the lies

she's tried by way of appeasement, truth
kicks. If it isn't her, it's another
more or less the same and the same smooth
release as he strips her of the love
they've made layer by layer. It soothes
knowing her shoulders carry that suffering
as well as her own. He can play doctors
with a back already sliced and knotted

with scars if he wants. Breaking what's broken
hardly counts, whether it gets him off
or not. He'll leave her alone to soak
clean for a week now at least, to soften
the thought of him to a drowsy smoke
after the showers she'll soon be offering
her wounds. There's a point at which the pain
can't get worse than having to explain it.

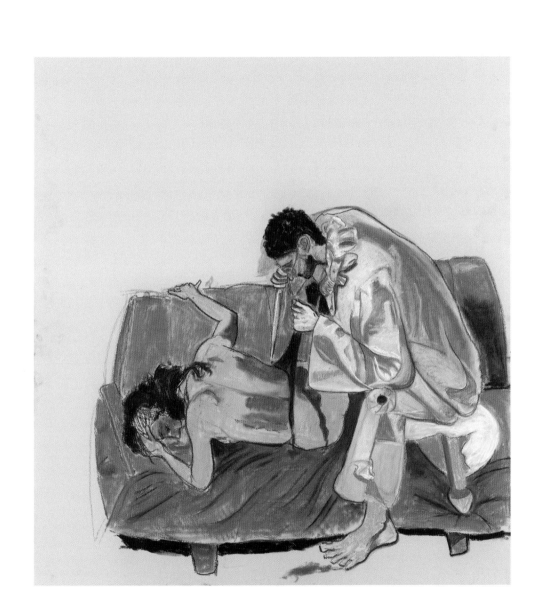

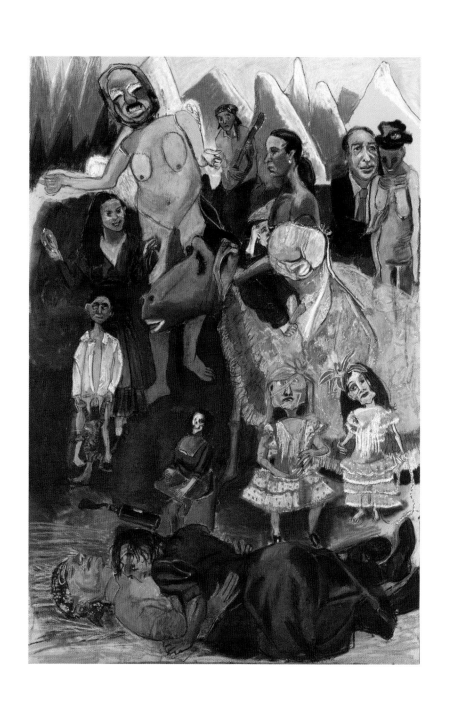

Do You Remember an Inn, Miranda?

On the mountain road with a bitter edge
to the breeze in summer and worse to come
for the muleteers and the local farmers
it's there or nowhere. The maids with necks
at unlikely angles remain at odds
to the rest whose footprints make no impression
on days the snow's on the slither down
from the higher ground. Their resistance matches
the couple found in the stable up
to their bollocks, bottle of tarry red
on its side, the grin they were stuck with caught
on the needles as they rattle the forest
against its ridge. When the tourists come
there are times they'll hear what the lovers paid
the guitarist for in the gap between
their attempts to talk and their breath. They'll stop
for a second, listen, and find it vanishes
when they do. There are times they'll see,
or at least remember by proxy, thinking
they've seen, the dancers with faces plastered
with chalk and powder, again dissolving
before they're trapped there. A stink of animals
rises too from the meadows miles
from the nearest stables, a legacy
born, or reborn, with the same in mind
as the woman who just appeared on horseback
protecting life with her frozen body
until the bar-keeps could prise it free
and she lost herself in a dream, a smother
of wine. A cross and a scrape of earth
are as much as anyone gets to guide them
towards the rubble and bone they left
for the passing trade and the mountain road.

Playground

A gang of girls parade their rifles
under a propeller's chunnering topple
and lurch. A mother has her clothes scorched
from her body blindfolding her daughter from the day
with her hands. It happens like a sandstorm lapping
years off a bone, appears from a stunned
calm and a crowd who stop singing
their hymns half-way through, dissolving
from assemblies to the schoolyard. The screams
come in instalments then stretch the coma
thin. The blind side of a door
waits for the sirens and the fires to wake
before it falls apart, pulling
one of the worldlier boys from blowing
his teacher's cock. The crack of a token
shot pisses at the floating planes
balanced on the verge of the first bombs
to stagger down. A ragged dawn
said as much, but it's muttered the same
plenty of times and turned up empty-
clawed. They're bored of the warnings now

they finally matter and the forecasts merge
with a truth discovering what it wants
to be. A second bullet pecks
a hole in the blue, blinding it and hoping
it might last. It's as bright as a burst
of glass though, glowing through the blasts
puffing brick-dust and plaster. Specks
continue to magnify into the nagging drone
of planes. The view remains true
to the maps slapped up back at base
trusting today was good to go
with the whole horizon and hereafter to hammer
flat. Ecstatic in their way, they float
before they fall, hang their fury
on a thermal, their weight airborne and then a world
somersaulting into ghost-masks again
and again. One of the girls grabs
an axe as an anchor against impact
while a man who doesn't move a muscle
lolls with his head in his lap as they hit.

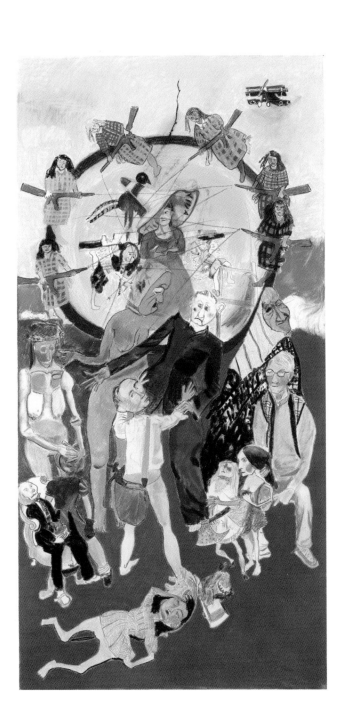

Taking Liberties: Retelling Rego

Owen Lowery

Rego Retold is the result of several years of fascination and poetic engagement with the work of Dame Paula Rego. Following an initial introduction by Anthony Rudolf, I began writing essays and poems about the dazzling world of colour and drama that Rego's pictures represent, responding both to their energy and to the stories behind them. In part, the basis for the ekphrastic response my poems provide to four decades of images exploring subjects as diverse as Charlotte Brontë's *Jane Eyre*, the Virgin Mary, and illegal abortion, is the open invitation provided by the artist's interest in narrative, her belief that 'Every picture tells a story as they say. Otherwise there's no point'.[1]

The simplicity with which Paula Rego expresses herself is deceptive, and should not mask the technical accomplishment of her work, or be regarded as an indication that everything she creates is exclusively narrative in nature; but it does offer a point at which poetry can begin to access the artist's work. In her essay on the importance of 'automatic narrative' in Rego's work, Fiona Bradley contends that the artist does not always begin the creative process with a definite narrative direction in mind, and does not simply illustrate the stories and scenarios to which she is drawn, but re-imagines them, citing *The Maids* as an example:

> Re-imagining the daughter as a little girl, she locks her into a deadly embrace with one maid. The other [maid] steals up on the older woman with what could almost be a tentative caress. In the picture's general air of foreboding and expectation, the threatening fingers of the branches of the tree outside seem the only thing

able to hint to the viewer what might really be going on.[2]

A similar process is apparent in Rego's illustrated *Jane Eyre*, in which literal response and imaginative transformation co-exist. *Girl Reading at Window* does not deviate from Charlotte Brontë's original text, depicting the first-person narrator sitting on a window seat with a book on her knee, as described by the author. *Loving Bewick*, on the other hand, reaches beyond the text, by portraying Jane in an embrace with one of the birds about which she has been reading, an arrangement that also occurs in Rego's reactions to the Jewish legend of the dybbuk. As Marina Warner reflects, this polarity extends to the finer details of the artist's illustrations, and arises from an interest in the fantastic that is common to both Rego and Brontë:

> Charlotte Brontë and Paula Rego share an imaginative ardour that abolishes the veil between what takes place in fact or in fantasy. As storytellers, they really are kith and kin: Rego reproduces the psychological drama in the book through subjective distortions of scale, cruel expressiveness of gesture and frown, and disturbingly stark contrasts of light and welling shadows.[3]

At the heart of this mutual connection is the dynamic drama associated with human relationships, in all their strangeness, and in the familiarity that makes them such a fitting subject for poetic re-exploration, not so much reversing the transition from written to visual text, but developing it further. John McEwen's awareness of Rego's ability to strike a chord with her audience focuses on the female perspective, but his argument can be successfully applied on a more general basis:

> It is the great appeal of Paula's art that she reveals us to our most shameful selves in this way and, more particularly, how she reveals women to themselves, for she depicts the 'human comedy' from a female point of view. She answers back, she tells the truth – sometimes the unpleasant truth – in her art.[4]

McEwen supports his claim by referring to the series of paintings about the *Red Monkey* that Rego began in the early 1980s, but he could just as easily have cited the *Jane Eyre* illustrations. *Rego Retold* includes poems based on six of these images, beginning with *Come to Me*, in which the protagonist is depicted kneeling and clenching her fists, with her facial expression heightened into the extreme anguish of a recognisably human predicament. Having heard Edward Rochester's physical and psychic cry for help, Jane is forced to decide between the life, love, and pain from which she has walked away, and the future offered by her newfound financial independence following the death of her uncle. The familiarity of this dilemma provides the entry point for my poem about the image, though the opening two tercets describe the point at which Jane's struggle has been resolved in Rochester's favour:

> Knowing as much as Jane does
> of life before inferno
> cleansed it from inside its lust

> has to be part of the turn
> she makes and yet doesn't make
> freely.

The narrative aspect of the Rego illustration has been developed, adding a new layer to the intertextual discourse in which the illustrated version of *Jane Eyre* takes part. Just as Rego's images do far more than simply reflect Charlotte Brontë's novel, my poem 'Come to Me' both draws on the visual stimulus, the immediate drama of vibrant red flames and an inky black dress, and reads into and out from the picture.

Writing the poem with the advantage of being able to reference the Brontë text, as well as the Rego image, allows the figure of Jane to become a visual and a psychological phenomenon, a complex of physical and less obvious attributes and attitudes. A fresh perspective is provided, that of a third-person observer and speaker, rather than that of the first-person heroine of Brontë's novel, or that of the visual artist. Jane can be considered and reflected upon as a character, a protagonist, with a past, a present, and a future, and as a composition of light and shade, and a response can be created which moves between these temporal stages and unfolds over time. Consequently, while the portrait of Jane in Rego's *Come to Me* is locked in its moment, the corresponding poem is able to look back towards Edward Rochester's previous marriage and consider the influence this might have on the present:

> The hold

> still of His wedding unearths
> the jasmine smells of moonlight
> on bedsheets and the split surf

wriggled in the sand of tuned
bodies.

A similar dialogue between narratives that develop
in three distinct phases occurs in the poems that I have
written in response to Rego's Father Amaro pictures.
This series takes as its subject José Maria de Eça de
Queiróz's novel *The Crime of Father Amaro*, in which the
title character is a priest in a provincial town who falls
in love and begins a sexual relationship with Amélia,
his landlady's daughter. Amélia's death following the
killing of her and Amaro's illegitimate child provides
Rego with the opportunity to interpret Queiróz's novel
in political as well as literal terms, as a woman reacting
to the suffering of other women, and that of their
children. Perhaps, to an even greater extent than *Jane
Eyre*, the artist's Father Amaro images take on a deep
personal resonance, not least because the novel is
reported to have been a favourite of her father's. The
pictures align themselves with a definite cause, though
not at the expense of objectivity, as she attempts to
understand Amaro's motivations and obsessions, rather
than simply depicting him as an epitome of patriarchal
domination, clumsiness, and cruelty. This balance is
achieved despite what John McEwen identifies as a
sense of injustice on Rego's part that extends to
English, as well as Portuguese, society and institutions:

> The Slade may have the smartest of art schools
> but in its male domination – albeit typical of the
> time – it could echo Portugal. Paula particularly
> disapproved of the way women were not treated
> as equals, and the fact that rich girls were
> admitted at the expense of poor ones in the hope
> that they would support struggling young male
> artists by marrying them.[5]

The effect, in the Amaro series, is a complex of
compositional and psychological relationships and
perspectives that shifts from one picture to another. In
The Company of Women, the priest is presented as a boy-
man, reclining in a dress among the maids and
domestic servants by whom he was often dressed as a
child. This portrayal allows and encourages a number
of different interpretations and narratives, while
ensuring that Amaro's self-indulgence and weakness
remain apparent. Elsewhere in the series, less
ambiguous images confront the implications of the
priest's crime. *Looking Out* portrays a young woman
standing barefooted, looking out through a window,
with one foot on a low stool and her back to the viewer
– a simple but powerful demonstration not only of
Amélia's social isolation in the wake of her pregnancy,
but of female subjugation on a wider basis, in Portugal
and under the Catholic Church.

In approaching Rego's Father Amaro series, I was
therefore keen to preserve, or at least not distort, the
artist's multi-faceted approach. In this sense, my Father
Amaro poems have had to tread even more carefully
than my Jane Eyre poems. My poem in response to *The
Company of Women* combines description of the corresponding image with psychological, philosophical,
religious, and sexual speculation in an attempt to
represent ambivalent suggestiveness:

> Any resistance
>
> he might've had disentangles
> an indulgence consistent with the lizard child
> curled inside the man. He chooses
> now to fold the wound in his side
> in the weeping linen of his blouse.

119

In *Jane Eyre*, reinvention is integral to the relationship between the original novel, the artist's reactions, and my poems, and the same is true in relation to *The Crime of Father Amaro*. Once again, the story changes as it is subjected to Rego's creative imagination, until it becomes 'her own retelling, embroidered in her mind's eye and fleshed out by her own perspective on the world'.[6] The artist adds 'episodes and characters of her own',[7] one of the most powerful and visually dramatic examples of which is the work titled *Angel*, in which the single figure of a woman occupies the centre of a vertical composition. Wearing metallic and bronze colours, she holds a sword in her right hand, and squeezes a sponge in her left hand, as if she has recently performed a castration. This figure does not appear in the original novel, but becomes an embodiment of justice, of the need to correct a colossal wrong. The outrage and strength of this picture are also registered in my corresponding poem, in the opening stanza of which they give rise to a combination of description and speculation, elaborating on the pictorial and compositional theme, as well as the narrative possibilities of the image:

A face reflecting what it reads in us
prepares to deliver with either hand
the language riding on a sword's tongue,
or the curious blend of wine and gall
drooling from a squeeze of testicular sponge,
something for the hollowing shout, the hunger
in a lover, a mind instantly enthralled
by a promise sweeter than it was long
enough to taste.

The redemptive figure, as encountered in my poem, becomes more overtly Christian than is perhaps the case in Rego's picture, building on the symbolic potential of the sword and the sponge, with the latter being associated with the sponge from which the crucified Christ was given gall, or vinegar. However, the force of the image, both in visual terms, and in those of the poem, far exceeds religious and doctrinal boundaries. The angelic presence allows the artist to intervene directly in the narrative of Father Amaro, and that of women in general, a tendency born out of the same passionate and undeniable empathy evident in her series of pictorial depictions of illegal abortion. Produced in reaction to the failure of the Portuguese referendum of 1998 to legalise abortion, these images leave no doubt as to the perceived consequences of the decision, offering stark interiors, female subjects crouched over plastic buckets, or cramped within the confines of their picture frames.

Just as the abortion series has political as well as personal and artistic significance, the continuing social relevance of Rego's work is also reflected in her *Two Women Being Stoned*. As with her earlier, more abstract composition, *Salazar Vomiting the Homeland*, the picture's title is uncompromising and unafraid of tackling its subject head-on, but the greater realism, and the accurate attention to figure, of *Two Women being Stoned* perhaps render this work more immediately accessible. As with so many of the narratives to which Paula Rego turns and returns, the scenario imagined, or recreated, in *Two Women Being Stoned* undergoes a degree of transformation that makes it far more than a replication of the original source, the political fact of female repression and punishment. The two women, who appear at the centre of the picture, are portrayed in modern Western clothes, and are loaded with symbolic and artistic signification. The woman in the foreground stoops in a bright red dress, invoking the traditional colour worn by Catholic martyrs. The second female figure, in the background, has her arms raised in the manner of the white-shirted witness of the execution depicted in Francisco Goya's *The Third of May 1808*. The artist therefore provides an indication that the spectacle of the stoning has repercussions that are not confined to the time and place of the activity. The brutal execution of women in Pakistan or Afghanistan equates to the brutal execution of women everywhere.

Rather than beginning with a description of what Rego's image achieves, my poem on the subject opens with an affirmation that the subjects of the picture are real people, individuals with personal histories and lives beyond what happens to them:

> Who they are and what their sins were
> matters beneath the dust and blood
> of their appointed day, each thud
> aimed through the clamour and a din
>
> of birds.

The ambition is to lift the two victims from a painterly presentation seemingly influenced by classical and neo-classical history painting, and to add movement to the deliberately stiff and statuesque depiction of an act as clumsy as it is barbaric. Having recognised the humanity of the women, my poem turns to the manner in which they are part of a long history of repression, awarding equivalent status of martyrs beheaded on the scaffolds of Tudor monarchies, and implying, just as the picture does, that the West is far from innocent of brutal execution. A link is established between British history and the parched and dusty Eastern and Middle Eastern environments in which the practice of stoning still occurs:

> Scarlet, the hackle dipped
> in war and then paraded calm,
> or the moment majesty's arms
> drop for the axe knowing the rip
>
> a dress steeped in martyred colour
> makes in time, help frame a contrast
> with what thousands of years of sun
> does to anywhere green.

Possibilities not necessarily immediately suggested by the image emerge. The drama shifts from its frozen present. Stones and wounds explode, bringing the scene to life, while preserving the visual intensity of the picture:

> The dirt stage spits and flaps
> its protests of dust at dulling blows.
>
> [...] Once grazes
> and gashes snap open like shells
>
> and flashes of why, it's a shoot
> on a Sunday afternoon. Shapes
> are hit and shatter. Dresses scrape
> and earrings peck at their neutral
> gleam with nicks and smearings.

The poem and the picture, or the picture and the poem, can therefore be seen to interact in the name of a new narrative, one that develops outside of either medium, one that remains precisely relevant to our understanding of the condition and position of women in the twenty-first century, and one that I hope fulfils some of Rego's ambitions in relation to working with narratives of any kind:

My favourite themes are power games and hier-archies […] If the story is 'given' I take liberties with it to make it conform to my own experi-ences, and to be outrageous […] Above all, though, I want to work with stories which emerge as I go along. It is something I have done in the past, and now I wish to do exactly that.[8]

Notes

1   Paula Rego, in *Paula Rego: Telling Tales*, directed and produced by Jake Auerbach (Jake Auerbach Films Ltd, 2009).

2   Fiona Bradley, 'Automatic Narrative', in Fiona Bradley, Judy Collins, Paula Rego, Ruth Rosengarten and Vic Willing, *Paula Rego* (London: Tate Gallery Publishing, 1997), p. 12.

3   Marina Warner, 'An Artist's Dreamland: *Jane Eyre* through Paula Rego's Eyes', in Paula Rego, *Jane Eyre* (London: Enitharmon Editions, first published in 2003, this edition 2005), p. 10.

4   John McEwen, *Paula Rego* (London: Phaidon Press, 3rd edn, 2008), p. 17.

5   McEwen, *Paula Rego*, p. 46.

6   Paula Rego, *Paula Rego* (Madrid: Museo Nacional Centro de Arte Reina Sofia, 2007), p. 54.

7   Rego, *Paula Rego*, p. 54.

8   McEwen, *Paula Rego*, p. 138.

Image Credits

All works by Paula Rego

In the Garden, 1986
Acrylic on paper on canvas
150 × 150 cm
Copyright the artist, courtesy Marlborough Fine Art, London

Girl Lifting Up her Skirt to a Dog, 1986
Acrylic on paper
80 × 60 cm
Copyright the artist, courtesy Marlborough Fine Art, London

Prey, 1986
Acrylic on paper on canvas
150 × 150 cm
Copyright the artist, courtesy Marlborough Fine Art, London

Looking Back, 1987
Acrylic on paper on canvas
150 × 150 cm
Saatchi Collection, London
Copyright the artist, courtesy Marlborough Fine Art, London

Snare, 1987
Acrylic on paper on canvas
150 × 150 cm
British Council
Copyright the artist, courtesy Marlborough Fine Art, London

Departure, 1988
Acrylic on paper on canvas
213.4 × 152.4 cm
Copyright the artist, courtesy Marlborough Finc Art, London

The Family, 1988
Acrylic on paper on canvas
213.4 × 213.4 cm.
Saatchi Collection, London
Copyright the artist, courtesy Marlborough Fine Art, London

Joseph's Dream, 1990
Acrylic on paper on canvas
183 × 122 cm
Private Collection
Copyright the artist, courtesy Marlborough Fine Art, London

Time – Past and Present, 1990–1991
Acrylic on paper on canvas
183 × 183 cm
Copyright the artist, courtesy Marlborough Fine Art, London

The First Mass in Brazil, 1993
Acrylic on canvas
130 × 180 cm
Private Collection
Copyright the artist, courtesy Marlborough Fine Art, London

Sleeper, 1994
Pastel on canvas
120 × 160 cm
Private Collection
Copyright the artist, courtesy Marlborough Fine Art, London

Moth, 1994
Pastel on canvas
160 × 120 cm
Private Collection
Copyright the artist, courtesy Marlborough Fine Art, London

Bride, 1994
Pastel on canvas
120 × 160 cm
Tate Collection, London
Copyright the artist, courtesy Marlborough Fine Art, London

Target, 1995
Pastel on canvas
160 × 120 cm
Copyright the artist, courtesy Marlborough Fine Art, London

Sit, 1994
Pastel on canvas
160 × 120 cm
Private Collection
Copyright the artist, courtesy Marlborough Fine Art, London

Snow White with her Stepmother, 1995
Pastel on paper mounted on aluminium
178 × 150 cm
Whitworth Art Gallery, Manchester
Copyright the artist, courtesy Marlborough Fine Art, London

Snow White on the Prince's Horse, 1995
Pastel on paper mounted on aluminium
160 × 120 cm
Private Collection
Copyright the artist, courtesy Marlborough Fine Art, London

Two Women Being Stoned, 1995
Pastel on canvas
150 × 150 cm
Copyright the artist, courtesy Marlborough Fine Art, London

Love, 1995
Pastel on paper mounted on aluminium
120 × 160 cm
Copyright the artist, courtesy Marlborough Fine Art, London

Love II, The Dybbuk, 1999
Pen, ink and watercolour
29.5 × 41.6 cm
Copyright the artist, courtesy Marlborough Fine Art, London

Geppetto Washing Pinocchio, 1995
Pastel on paper mounted on aluminium
170 × 150 cm
Private Collection
Copyright the artist, courtesy Marlborough Fine Art, London

The Company of Women, 1997
Pastel on paper mounted on aluminium
170 × 130 cm
Collection of the artist
Copyright the artist, courtesy Marlborough Fine Art, London

The Ambassador of Jesus, 1998
Pastel on paper mounted on aluminium
100 × 80 cm
Saatchi Collection, London
Copyright the artist, courtesy Marlborough Fine Art, London

Looking Out, 1997
Pastel on paper mounted on aluminium
180 × 130 cm
Private Collection
Copyright the artist, courtesy Marlborough Fine Art, London

Perch, 1997
Pastel on paper mounted on aluminium
120 × 100 cm
Private Collection
Copyright the artist, courtesy Marlborough Fine Art, London

The Coop, 1998
Pastel on paper mounted on aluminium
150 × 150 cm
Private Collection
Copyright the artist, courtesy Marlborough Fine Art, London

Angel, 1998
Pastel on paper mounted on aluminium
100 × 80 cm
Collection of the artist
Copyright the artist, courtesy Marlborough Fine Art, London

The Betrothal: Lessons: The Shipwreck, after 'Marriage à la Mode' by Hogarth, 1999
Pastel on paper mounted on aluminium
Tate Collection, London

    Part I (left panel)
    150 × 160 cm

Part II (central panel)
150 × 90 cm

Part III (right panel)
150 × 160 cm
Copyright the artist, courtesy Marlborough Fine Art, London

Pietà, 2002
Pastel on paper mounted on aluminium
54 × 52 cm
Chapel of the Palacio de Belém, Lisbon
Copyright the artist, courtesy Marlborough Fine Art, London

Assumption, 2002
Pastel on paper mounted on aluminium
54 × 52 cm
Chapel of the Palacio de Belém, Lisbon
Copyright the artist, courtesy Marlborough Fine Art, London

Adoration, 2002
Pastel on paper mounted on aluminium
54 × 52 cm
Chapel of the Palacio de Belém, Lisbon
Copyright the artist, courtesy Marlborough Fine Art, London

Lamentation, 2002
Pastel on paper mounted on aluminium
54 × 52 cm
Chapel of the Palacio de Belém, Lisbon
Copyright the artist, courtesy Marlborough Fine Art, London

Come to Me, 2001–2002
Coloured lithograph
99.5 × 67 cm
Edition of 35
Copyright the artist, courtesy Marlborough Fine Art, London

Mr Rochester, 2002
Lithograph
89.5 × 67 cm
Edition of 35
Copyright the artist, courtesy Marlborough Fine Art, London

Schoolroom, 2001–2002
Lithograph on stone
62.5 × 88 cm
Edition of 35
Copyright the artist, courtesy Marlborough Fine Art, London

La Ligue des Rats, 2002
Lithograph on stone
56 × 46 cm
Edition of 35
Copyright the artist, courtesy Marlborough Fine Art, London

Getting Ready for the Ball, 2001–2002
Coloured lithograph on 3 sheets
82.5 × 180 cm overall
Edition of 35
Copyright the artist, courtesy Marlborough Fine Art, London

Biting, 2002
Coloured lithograph
90 × 62 cm
Edition of 35
Copyright the artist, courtesy Marlborough Fine Art, London

Snow White Swallows the Poisoned Apple, 1995
Pastel on paper mounted on aluminium
170 × 150 cm
Saatchi Collection, London
Copyright the artist, courtesy Marlborough Fine Art, London

Olga, 2003
Pastel on paper mounted on aluminium
160 × 120 cm
Copyright the artist, courtesy Marlborough Fine Art, London

Feeding, 2005
Etching and aquatint with hand colouring
57.5 × 48.7 cm
Edition of 25
Copyright the artist, courtesy Marlborough Fine Art, London

Fame, 2005
Etching and aquatint with hand colouring
57.5 × 48.7 cm
Edition of 25
Copyright the artist, courtesy Marlborough Fine Art, London

Prince Pig and his First Bride, 2006
Lithograph
65.5 × 73 cm
Edition of 35
Copyright the artist, courtesy Marlborough Fine Art, London

The Psychiatrist, 2011
Pastel on paper
138 × 102 cm
Copyright the artist, courtesy Marlborough Fine Art, London

Dame with the Goat's Foot (I), 2011–2012
Pastel on paper
137 × 102 cm
Copyright the artist, courtesy Marlborough Fine Art, London

At the Table, 2012
Pastel on paper
72 × 75 cm
Copyright the artist, courtesy Marlborough Fine Art, London

The Last Feed, 2012
Pastel on paper
159.7 × 120.2 cm
Copyright the artist, courtesy Marlborough Fine Art, London

Flayed, 2012
Pastel on paper
130.3 × 120.6 cm
Copyright the artist, courtesy Marlborough Fine Art, London

Do You Remember an Inn, Miranda?, 2012
Pastel on paper
180 × 120 cm
Copyright the artist, courtesy Marlborough Fine Art, London

Playground, 2012–13
Pastel on paper
240 × 120 cm
Copyright the artist, courtesy Marlborough Fine Art, London

Acknowledgements

This book would not have been possible without the encouragement, generosity, and friendship of Anthony Rudolf and Dame Paula Rego, nor, of course, without Paula's fantastic catalogue of images. It is their dramas, narratives, savage wit, and humanity that have inspired my poems. Thank you so much for everything.

I am very grateful to Paula Rego's gallery, Marlborough Fine Art, London, for their help and support, in particular Frankie Rossi and Mary Miller. Also a big thank you to Francesco Dama at the gallery for his care and diligence in finding the best reproductions and providing the image credits.

I must thank Michael Schmidt, Helen Tookey, Alice Mullen, and everybody else at Carcanet for their patience and hard work, and for producing such a beautiful book. Professor Jon Glover, at the University of Bolton, is another to whom I am greatly indebted for everything he has done to get me writing in the first place.

Thank you to my mother, Sybil, for plenty of secretarial assistance and a background of good books.

Alison Boyle and Arts Council England have played a vital role in funding the research, development, and production of *Rego Retold*. It is a huge privilege to benefit from such generous support.

I am equally appreciative of the role that Unlimited are playing in helping to fund performances of my work, including poems from *Rego Retold*.

The Regain Sports Charity for tetraplegics who have suffered sporting injuries has been invaluable too. Regain has been there for me for more than a decade, and has provided my last three adapted computers, including my current Apple iMac, with which all of the poems included in *Rego Retold* were written.

Above all, I want to thank my wife, Jayne, not just for what she means to my writing, but for what she means to me, and for coping with being married to a poet. You will always be at the heart of everything I do. *Rego Retold* is the latest in so many wonderful steps that we continue to take together.

Owen Lowery
2014